THE **PROPHETIC THROUGH** THE **EYE** OF THE **EAGLE**

LINDA MORALES

Inspiring Voices®
A Service of **Guideposts**

Inspiring Voices books may be ordered through booksellers or by contacting:

Inspiring Voices
1663 Liberty Drive
Bloomington, IN 47403
www.inspiringvoices.com
1-(866) 697-5313

ISBN: 978-1-4624-0141-3 (sc)
ISBN: 978-1-4624-0140-6 (e)

Library of Congress Control Number: 2012937623

Printed in the United States of America

Inspiring Voices rev. date: 04/18/2012

CONTENTS

This chapter explains and elaborates on the order and functions of each of the ministry callings as written in Ephesians 4:11-13.

This chapter explains and gives understanding of moving in the Prophetic Anointing, as well as, going into depth of the gifting of "the Word of Knowledge"

This chapter enables us to have understanding of symbols, colors, and messages God is trying to speak to us through dreams. Just as God gave Prophet Daniel in Daniel 1:17 "understanding in all visions and dreams."

This chapter explains moving in Prophecy as spoken in I Corinthians 14:3 "for comfort, edification, and exhortation," for the past, the present, and the future.

This chapter goes into the tactics of our enemy; without knowing the enemy how can we fight the good fight of faith.

This chapter has a few teachings revealing the revelations of the Word of God as spoken of in Ephesians 3:5.

ACKNOWLEDGEMENTS

All Glory, Honor, and Praise goes to My Lord and Saviour, Jesus Christ who changed my life and continues to change my life on my journey from Glory to Glory. I want to thank Jesus for my beautiful husband, Apostle Tito Morales for how the Lord has used him in my life to be the Prophet of God that God has called me to be. I also want to thank Rick and Prophet Annette Ellspermann for their hard work in correcting and editing this book for God's Glory. Thank you.

PREFACE

As the Spirit of God moved across the face of the waters, God the Father through the Lord Jesus Christ created all things. In six days created He everything and on the seventh day He rested; not because He was tired, but because He is All Powerful, Almighty, He is the Great I Am; He is Jehovah, the Glorious God and He had finished it all. Remember what the Word of God says that when He created man, He created him perfect. Genesis 1:27, "So God created man in His own image, in the image of God created he him; male and female created he them."

Jehovah God had created Adam perfect and He placed the Prophetic call on his life. God Almighty entrusted Adam to name every living creature. Genesis 2:19, 20, "And out of the ground the Lord God formed every beast of the field, and every fowl of the air; and brought them unto Adam to see what he would call them: and whatsoever Adam called every living creature, that was the name thereof. And Adam gave names to all cattle, and to the fowl of the air, and to every beast of the field; but for Adam there was not found an help meet for him." Adam had such an awesome relationship and communication with God the Father, God the Son, and with God the Holy Spirit, that they communed with him in the Garden of Eden. By having that tremendous relationship with God Almighty, Adam was able to move as a Prophet and name every living thing. The Word of God says that the Voice walked with him; the Voice is Jesus Christ, the Word of God. Genesis 3:8, 9, "And they heard the voice of the Lord God walking in the garden in the cool of the day: and Adam and His wife hid themselves from the presence of the Lord God amongst the trees of the garden. And the Lord God called unto Adam, and said unto him, "Where art thou?" Notice, that God the Father, God the Son, and God the Holy Spirit are always together in unity. God the Father having created Adam asked him, "Where art thou?" And Jesus Christ was the voice walking in the cool of the day and the Holy Spirit was the presence.

We need to understand that even though Jehovah God had created Adam perfect that when Adam sinned he did not fully complete the Prophetic call in his life. So God Almighty had to send the second Adam, Jesus Christ, to fulfill that Prophetic call. I Corinthians 15:45, "And so it is written, the first man Adam was made a living soul; the last Adam was made a quickening spirit." Jesus Christ, The Prophet, came to fulfill that Prophetic call that the first Adam did not complete and He restored the communication back between us and the Father. The Word of God says that He also called us to fulfill the Prophetic call or the calling that God has placed on our lives as the Word of God says in Ephesians 4:11-13. How many of us are ready to do that, or are we going to be like the first Adam and let someone else fulfill our Prophetic calling?

It is time we allow the Spirit of the Living God that dwells within us to Glorify, Magnify, and Lift up the name of the Lord Jesus Christ. If you want God to use you powerfully in the realm of the spirit as a Prophet of God or even with the prophetic anointing, let it be as you read this book that God opens up your eyes of understanding and brings forth the revelations of the Word of God and enlightening your understanding to know how to move in the realm of the spirit so mightily that you will know everyone by the spirit.

I pray this Apostolic Prayer over you, as the Apostle Paul had prayed over his disciples: "That the God of Our Lord Jesus Christ, the Father of glory, may give unto you the spirit of wisdom and revelation in the knowledge of him: The eyes of your understanding being enlightened; that you may know what is the hope of his calling, and what the riches of the glory of his inheritance in the saints, and what is the exceeding greatness of his power to us-ward who believe, according to the working of his mighty power, which he wrought in Christ, when he raised him from the dead, and set him at his own right hand in the heavenly place, far above all principality, and power, and might, and dominion, and every name that is named, not only in this world, but also in that which is to come: And hath put all things under his feet, and gave him to be the head over all things to the church, which is his body, the fullness of him that filleth all in all." (Ephesians 1:17-23) Also, I pray for each of you as you are reading this book and are truly hungry for the things of God for His Glory, that by His Holy Spirit you will receive an impartation of the prophetic anointing in your life that you will be used miraculously by God. Let us be true Watchmen for God's people as God has called us to be through His Word in Ezekiel 3:17, "Son of man, I have made thee a watchman unto the house of Israel: therefore hear the word at my mouth and give them warning from me." Let us be as the eagles soaring high in the presence of the Lord; separating ourselves unto Him. Let us not only live in the Spirit, but let us walk in the Spirit.

It is time we put our hand to the plow....doing the work of the Lord, building God's Kingdom not ours. That is the reason God put it in my spirit to write this book to help all those that are ready to be used by the Lord. It is time we realize what the Word of God says that this is like a race and we need to get on the right track. Luke 9:62 says, "And Jesus said unto him, No man, having put his hand to the plough, and looking back, is fit for the kingdom of God." We cannot delay any longer for the time is short and the Spirit of the Living God will be taking those of us following the ways of the Lord up in the rapture for the wedding banquet. I Thessalonians 4:16, 17, "For the Lord himself shall descend from heaven with a shout, with the voice of the archangel, and with the trump of God: and the dead in Christ shall rise first. Then we which are alive and remain shall be caught up together with them in the clouds, to meet the Lord in the air: and so shall we ever be with the Lord."

When we step into the call of God that He has for our lives, that is when the fullness of His joy comes into our lives. Jesus also said in His Word, blessed is he who when I come I find him doing the will of my Father. The Heart of God is Souls; and the Bible says in Proverbs 11:30: "....and he that winneth souls is wise." When we tell people about Jesus Christ, the Word of God, the Spirit of the Living God within us draws men unto Jesus.

INTRODUCTION

Blessings in the Glorious name of Our Lord Jesus Christ to each and everyone that is reading this book. I believe if you are reading this book, it is because you are hungry for the things of God, you are looking for more, you want the deep calling unto deep and you want the understanding of what the spiritual realm is all about. This is what it is all about; knowing your God, Jesus Christ, knowing who you are in Him, and knowing and moving in the realm of the spirit in such a dimension that you have that intimacy with your God and He uses you for His glory. When you have that relationship with the Lord Jesus Christ so intimately He will reveal the secret things unto you.

However, many of us are still going by what the law says in Deuteronomy 29:29, "The secret things belong unto the Lord our God: but those things which are revealed belong unto us and to our children for ever, that we may do all the words of this law." If you understand your God and become the Prophet of God that He is calling you to be, you can move into what God says unto us, the Prophets, as He said to the Prophet Jeremiah in Jeremiah 33:3, "Call unto me, and I will answer thee, and shew thee great and mighty things, which thou knowest not." That is the purpose of this book. Just like the Prophets in the Old Testament like Samuel, Elijah and Elisha they all had prophet schools to teach and train the people the things of God. Here again, you might be thinking you can't make someone a Prophet of God; this is true, just as a pineapple can't be a banana, nor an apple a pear, the same it is for our calling from God. The gifts and the callings for each one of us comes from God like the Word of God says in Romans 11:29, "For the gifts and calling of God are without repentance." However, we need the revelations and understanding of the Word of God, to understand the things of the spirit. Like Jesus said in John 4:23, "But the hour cometh, and now is, when the true worshippers shall worship the Father in spirit and in truth: for the Father seeketh such to worship him."

Understanding the revelations of the Word of God and understanding the spiritual principles is exciting. Our lives are fulfilled when we accept Jesus Christ as Our Lord and Savior and step into the call of God for our lives. Remember the parable that Jesus told of the giving of the talents. Starting in Matthew chapter 25 verse 15 thru 23; where to one He gave five talents and when that person used what God had given him, God said "Well done, good and faithful servant; thou hast been faithful over a few things, I will make thee ruler over many things: enter thou into the joy of thy lord." Notice that is when we truly get the Joy of the Lord in our lives and will know that our lives are being fulfilled when we are doing what God called us to do. This is why we need to understand the spiritual realm and the spiritual principles behind the Word of God. The Word of God tells us that we need to live and walk in the spirit; in other words we need to no longer walk in the soulish realm which is the mind, will, and emotions. Zechariah 4:6, "Not by might, nor by power, but by my spirit, says the Lord of hosts." We need to live in the spirit and to know each other by the spirit not by the soulish realm. This may sound hard but listen to this by the spirit not by our fleshly ears: our husbands, our wives, our kids, our jobs, and so on can take us to hell but Jesus Christ takes us to heaven. II Corinthians 5:16 says, "Wherefore henceforth know we no man after the flesh: yea, though we have known Christ after the flesh, yet now henceforth know we him no more." When John the Baptist saw Jesus coming he didn't say hey look here comes my cousin; no he said, "Behold the Lamb of God, which taketh away the sin of the world." (John 1:29) Moving in the spirit is an awesome adventure with the Lord Jesus and in order for God to use us powerfully we need to be full of the Word of God. John 3:34 says, "For he whom God hath sent speaketh the words of God: for God giveth not the Spirit by measure unto him," and the Spirit wants to lift up and Glorify the name of Jesus! Also, Hebrews 4:12 says that the Word of God "...is a discerner of the thoughts and intents of the heart." So, if you are ready for this spiritual adventure, I pray that even as you read this book that it will impart the revelations of the Word of God and open up your spiritual eyes to see and give you a hunger and a passion for the Word of God.

Walking and living separated for God is awesome, exciting, and you will be full of the joy of the Lord. The Prophets in the Old Testament moved mightily and they just had the Spirit of the Lord come upon them. These later days as Jesus Christ said the Later Glory will be greater than the Former Glory because the Spirit of the Living God is within us. How awesome it is for us that God the Father, thru Our Lord and Savior, Jesus Christ, has put His Spirit within us when we have accepted Jesus Christ as Our Lord and Saviour. I Corinthians 3:16; "Know ye not that ye are the temple of God, and that the Spirit of God dwelleth in you?" Remember that God the Father sent His son, Jesus, and Jesus sent the Holy Spirit, and the Holy Spirit sent forth the Apostles (Acts 13:2; Where it says "the Holy Ghost said, separate me Barnabas and Saul for the work whereunto I have called them."), and the Apostles send forth the Prophets, Evangelist, Pastors, and Teachers for the work of the Lord. So, if you are ready to go forward in the Lord…let's go. Have your bibles with you so you can search the scriptures for yourself. Let's be like the Bereans that Apostle Paul spoke of in the book of Acts 17:10, 11, "And the brethren immediately sent away Paul and Silas by night unto Berea; who coming thither went into the synagogue of the Jews. These were more noble than those in Thessalonica, in that they received the word with all readiness of mind, and searched the scriptures daily, whether those things were so." I am emphasizing this so we all have that intimate, personal relationship with Our God, Jesus Christ and know Him, the Word of God for ourselves!

GOD IS A GOD OF ORDER

Our God, the Creator of all the Heavens and the Earth, who put the stars in their place, who separated the vastness of the waters and the land, the one who created all the animals of the land, the sea, and the air, the creator of every living thing; Yes, this is Our God and He is a God of Order. You may say, "What does that mean?" Let me explain it in accordance with the Word of God. Everything God does is for a purpose and a plan and when God the Father does anything you will notice that His Son, Jesus Christ, and the Holy Spirit are always there because they are ONE.

After Jesus Christ died on the cross and rose from the dead; He came back to show Himself to the disciples for forty days. Acts 1:3, "To whom also he shewed himself alive after his passion by many infallible proofs, being seen of them forty days, and speaking of the things pertaining to the kingdom of God." There are several reasons why Jesus had to come back to show Himself to the disciples. First of all, the disciples were all backslidden; they had all gone back to fishing and doing what they use to do. Secondly, the disciples were all walking in the flesh and if Jesus had not come back in a bodily form they wouldn't have known Him; even before, like when Jesus walked on the water the disciples tried to say He was a ghost. (Matthew 14:26) Jesus had always told the disciples what was going to happen before time; He foretold, so, He came back to show them that everything He had spoken had come to pass and happened just as He had spoken. Fourthly, Jesus had to come back to explain to the disciples the protocols, the code of conduct, and the governments of Christ so that order could be established for the Body of Christ. Our Lord Jesus gave them understanding that when they received the Baptism of the Holy Spirit that by His power they would be able to fulfill the call of God in their lives in accordance with the Word of God for the five fold ministry. (Ephesians 4:8-13) Our Lord Jesus took this time to expound on Gods' Order that we, the church, could be built up on the right foundations. So that, we the church would be a Holy Temple, not made by hands. Ephesians 2:20 says, "And are built upon the foundation of the apostles and prophets, Jesus Christ himself being the chief corner stone." Jesus Christ is not only the chief corner stone but He is the First Apostle according to Hebrews 3:1, "Wherefore, holy brethren, partakers of the heavenly calling, consider the Apostle and High Priest of our profession, Christ Jesus."

The House of God needs to be in order as well as our own homes in order for the prophetic office and gifting to operate. Once order is established, God can bring forth deliverance and the Word of the Lord can come forward with revelation and holiness. If you notice from Genesis all the way to Matthew the pastors, the teachers, the evangelist, and even the prophets tried to bring people together in unity by fasting, praying, having conferences, etc. and it never worked. This is why Jesus Christ had to die on the cross and become the first Apostle, that order could be established by the five-fold ministry!! God shows us the importance of the Apostolic; that means spiritual fathers, coming in when His Word says in the last verse of the Old Testament in Malachi 4:6, "And He shall turn the heart of the fathers to the children, and the heart of the children to their fathers, lest I come and smite the earth with a curse."

The Apostolic brings discipline and order into the Body of Christ, which we need. Like the Apostle Paul says in I Corinthians 4:15, "For though ye have ten thousand instructors in Christ, yet have ye not many fathers: for in Christ Jesus I have begotten you through the gospel." We need the wisdom, guidance correction and chastisement that a father brings to our life. Many people try to dispute that the Apostles and the Prophets are for today; saying that Apostles were only for the time period while Jesus was here on the earth. If that were so, we would have to take out of the Bible 13 and possibly 14 books of the Bible because Apostle Paul came after Jesus Christ ascended. The Apostle Paul being inspired by the Spirit of the Living God, wrote the books of Romans, I and II Corinthians, Galatians, Ephesians, Philippians, Colossians, I and II Thessalonians, I and II Timothy, Titus, and Philemon, and possibly even Hebrews. We, Gentiles, need to bless the Lord for the

Apostle Paul because the Lord used him by the Spirit to draw us unto salvation through Jesus Christ.

When we build a house we must first lay a foundation; the same applies for the House of God according to Ephesians 2:20, as mentioned before, that the Apostles and Prophets are the foundation and Jesus Christ is the chief corner stone. Once the foundations are laid for a house we can begin to build; so also with God's House. Almost 1800 years ago the Apostles and the Prophets were taken out of the Church and when that happened the Spirit of Holiness also left because the bible is very clear in Ephesians 4:11-13 that it is only through the five-fold ministry that the Body of Christ, meaning us, are perfected. In Psalms 11:3 it says: "If the foundations be destroyed what can the righteous do?" Listen carefully to what that scripture says, read it again...; "If the foundations be destroyed what can the righteous do?" I have seen many people that have fallen out of the presence of God, that have gone back into doing the things of the world, and I have seen many marriages dissolved that I truly believe could have survived had they have been established on the right foundations. But when the foundations are destroyed it's hard to stand. Remember, the parable that Jesus gave in Matthew 7:24-27, "Therefore whosoever heareth these sayings of mine, and doeth them, I will liken him unto a wise man, which built his house upon a rock: and the rain descended, and the floods came, and the winds blew, and beat upon that house and it fell not: for it was founded upon a rock. And every one that heareth these sayings of mine, and doeth them not, shall be likened unto a foolish man, which built his house upon the sand: and the rain descended, and the floods came, and the winds blew, and beat upon that house and it fell: and great was the fall of it." That Rock is Jesus Christ and we have to build it His way not our way. I Corinthians 10:4, "And did all drink the same spiritual drink; for they drank of that spiritual Rock that followed them: and that Rock was Christ." So, we need to make sure we are in a five-fold ministry like the Word of God says in Ephesians 4:11, 12, and 13 that we may be perfected.

The Word of God says in I Corinthians 12:28, "And God hath set some in the church, first apostles, secondarily prophets, thirdly teachers, after that miracles then gifts of healings, helps governments, diversities of tongues." You will notice that the word says Apostles first and secondarily Prophets because that establishes the foundations.

Once, we establish ourselves in a true five-fold ministry, where God wants us to be, we need to understand our gifts and calling. We need to understand that any of the offices or callings of God whether it be Apostles, Prophets, Evangelist, Pastors, or Teachers are given by God. God puts it in our spirits what our gifts and calling are and then He will confirm it through a man or woman of God and then He will activate them. After Apostle Paul received the revelation of who Jesus Christ was and is, when he was on the road to Damascus in Acts chapter 9; God then sent Ananias, a man of God, to him to confirm his calling, to pray for him for deliverance, and for the baptism of the Holy Spirit. This activated the call of God for Apostle Paul's life. This is what an Apostle does. Jesus, Himself, could have removed the scales from Saul's, (later Apostle Paul) eyes but he chose to use man; another Apostle. Immediately, Apostle Paul separated himself unto the Lord to be taught by the Holy Spirit. Galatians 3:16-18, "To reveal his Son in me, that I might preach him among the heathen; immediately I conferred not with flesh and blood: Neither went I up to Jerusalem to them which were apostles before me; but I went into Arabia, and returned again unto Damascus. Then after three years I went up to Jerusalem to see Peter, and abode with him fifteen days." It was during this time that the Spirit of the Lord revealed to Apostle Paul that God had this calling on his life from the foundations of the world. Ephesians 1:4, "According as he hath chosen us in him before the foundation of the world, that we should be holy and without blame before him in love." Not only from the foundations of the world but He revealed to Apostle Paul that while he was in his mother's womb God had the Apostolic call on his life. Galatians 1:15, "But when it pleased God, who separated me from my mother's womb, and called me by his grace."

This was not only for the Apostle Paul's life; let's look at a few others. The Prophet Jeremiah's life; he too knew that his calling was even while he was in his mother's womb. Jeremiah 1:5, "Before I formed thee in the belly, I knew thee; and before thou camest forth out of the womb I sanctified thee, and I ordained thee a prophet unto the nations."

John the Baptist is another example. First of all, the angel Gabriel had told his father, Zacharias, before he was born that he would be a Prophet to prepare the way of the Lord. Luke 1:17, "And he shall go before him in the spirit and power of Elias, to turn the hearts of the fathers to the children, and the disobedient to the wisdom of the just; to make ready a people prepared for the Lord." Remember when Elisabeth was pregnant with John the Baptist and Mary being pregnant with Jesus came to her cousin's house; because the First Apostle, Jesus Christ, according to Hebrews 3:1 came in the presence of the Prophet, John the Baptist, the babe leaped in her womb because he was filled with the Holy Ghost and he received the anointing of a Prophet to do what God called him to do. Luke 1:41, "And it came to pass, that, when Elisabeth heard the salutation of Mary, the babe leaped in her womb; and Elisabeth was filled with the Holy Ghost." Again, this shows us how an Apostle activates, fills us and sends us out. When an Apostle is speaking our spirits should leap; mine does when I hear the revelations of the Word of God. Glory to God, Forever!

It is the same for the calling of THE PROPHET, Our Lord and Saviour, Jesus Christ. God the Father called Him from the foundations of the world and from the bowels of his mother as the Word of God says in Isaiah 49:1, 2: "Listen O isles, unto me; and hearken, ye people, from far; the Lord hath called me from the womb; from the bowels of my mother hath he made mention of my name. And he hath made my mouth like a sharp sword; in the shadow of his hand hath he hid me, and made me a polished shaft; in his quiver hath he hid me." Moses spoke of Jesus coming as THE PROPHET that would come and they would listen to Him. Read Deuteronomy 18:18, 19, "I will raise them up a Prophet from among their brethren, like unto thee, and will put my words in his mouth; and he shall speak unto them all that I shall command him. And it shall come to pass, that whosoever will not hearken unto my words which he shall speak in my name, I will require it of him." See, God calls us, He separates us, He refines us, and then He sends us out. The same way it was for Prophet Samuel, for Samson, and many, many others. So, when a Prophet or a man or woman of God tells you, God is calling you to be a Prophet or an Evangelist, or any one of the callings in a five-fold ministry this should quicken your spirit because God has already established it from the foundations of the world.

Many people when they receive a prophetic word of how God wants to use them mightily; immediately, they quit their jobs, their family is going hungry; they can't pay the rent....Why?....Because they didn't wait for time and season to come together. According to Deuteronomy

8:2, God, Himself, takes us into the wilderness to prove our character, to make sure we have all bitterness, unforgiveness, anger, lust, etc. out of our lives. Then Bamb, time and season come together and God will put us in favor with God and man. Doors will be open to minister to individuals, to churches, to leaders, to governments and nations and Jehovah Jireh, Our God, will supply for our needs. Not only do we need to wait on time and season to come together, we also need the heavens to be opened for us. Remember God called Abraham friend, He called Daniel beloved and Jesus Christ, when He was baptized the heavens were opened and the Spirit of God descended upon Him like a dove and God the Father spoke saying, "This is my beloved Son, in whom I am well pleased." (Matthew 3:17) God the Father called Jesus friend, He called Him, His Beloved, and He called Him, His Son. When God the Father spoke from heaven He was declaring to the heavens of the heavens, and to all the heavenly host, to Michael, the archangel, to Gabriel, the messenger angel, and to all in the third heaven that this is My Son and you shall listen to Him and obey what He speaks. God the Father was also speaking to the second heaven where satan, principalities and rulers of darkness dwell that they will submit all their power and authority unto My Son. And unto the first heaven and all that dwell within it God the Father was declaring that all power and authority and dominion were being given to His Son. It is the same for us, we need to know that God is calling us his friend, his beloved, and His son or His daughter and that the heavens be opened for us and that God the Father is declaring to the first, the second, and the third heaven to listen and be obedient to His Word being spoken through us. What God the Father is saying in this is for all the angels in the third heaven (and in the heavens of the heavens) that He is well pleased with us and all the angels have to heed to the Word of the Lord from your mouth. Like the Word of God says in Hebrews 1:13, 14, "But to which of the angels said he at any time, Sit on my right hand, until I make thine enemies thy footstool? Are they not all ministering spirits, sent forth to minister for them who shall be heirs of salvation." See when the heavens are opened for us and we declare the Word of the Lord the angels will go out and accomplish the Word of the Lord that we have spoken. Psalms 103:20, 21, "Bless the Lord, ye his angels that excel in strength, that do his commandments, hearkening unto the voice of his word. Bless ye the Lord, all ye his host; ye ministers of his, that do his pleasure." How awesome Our God is to have chosen us to speak His Word and the angels of the Lord heed to it!

We need to fully understand the ways of Our God; notice, God the Father, had just declared Jesus to be His Son and immediately after this, the Spirit led Jesus into the wilderness to be tested. Why? Because God always allows satan to have the first shot. When we receive a prophetic word from God, God will allow the enemy to come to see if we are going to stand believing what God has spoken to us. Notice in Luke 4:1-14 the very thing The Father had spoken to Jesus the enemy tested Him on. The devil said, "If, thou be the Son of God," the very word spoken by God the Father, the enemy will challenge. So, if a Prophet comes to prophesy to you about money and says that God is going to make you very rich; run, run, and go put your money in a secure place because God allows the enemy to have the first shot to see if we are going to stand and believe the Word of the Lord spoken through the Prophet.

When a man or woman of God speaks a prophetic word over your life it should quicken your spirit, however; if they are speaking from the soulish realm (that is the mind, will and emotions) it will not quicken your spirit. (May sound good to your flesh, but we need to move by the spirit.) We need to know and understand that when God allows the enemy to come against the prophetic word spoken to us, that God may use these tests to take us to a higher realm of the spirit. After passing the first test, God allows the devil to take Jesus up to a high mountain. Jesus again passing the second test; God allows the devil to come a third time to take Jesus up on a pinnacle of the temple, the highest point to prove that Jesus would stand on the Word. Notice, Jesus always spoke the Word to the enemy; He would say, "It is written." Jesus could have just said I am God and that is that, but even Our Master spoke what was written and already established in the heavens. So, if Jesus, Himself, spoke the written word of God, how much more we should. What we need to understand is in the Kingdom of God you never fail a test - you just keep taking it over and over and over until you pass it by standing on the Word of God. After Jesus passed all the tests, look what the Word of God says in verse 14...Jesus came down into Galilee with POWER!!! What God is showing us is when we pass the tests; meaning we don't allow our husbands, our wives, our kids, or any situation to move us, He will send us out with Power! Glory to God, Forever!

When God makes the call on your life, we still need to be trained up in the ways of God and understanding the spiritual realm. Let's look at Elisha when God made the call on his life. God told Elijah to go anoint Elisha to be the Prophet to take his place. I Kings 19:16, "...and Elisha the son of Shaphat of Abelmeholah shalt thou anoint to be a prophet in thy room." Then in verse 19, Elijah placed the mantle upon Elisha. I Kings 19:19, "So he departed thence, and found Elisha the son of Shaphat who was plowing with twelve yoke of oxen before him, and he with the twelfth; and Elijah passed by him, and cast his mantle upon him. This activated the calling of God in Prophet Elisha's life. Notice, first Elisha got his house in order, like we need to do, and then he went and ministered to Elijah. (Verses 20, 21) "And he left the oxen, and ran after Elijah, and said, "Let me, I pray thee, kiss my father and my mother, and then I will follow thee. And he said unto him, Go back again: for what have I done to thee? And he returned back from him, and took a yoke of oxen, and slew them, and boiled their flesh with the instruments of the oxen, and gave unto the people, and they did eat. Then he arose, and went after Elijah, and ministered unto him." Elisha had no problem humbling himself and being a servant unto the Prophet Elijah as he learned the ways of God and what it meant to be a Prophet. We can all learn from this! Many of us today want to fulfill our calls as Prophets, Evangelists, Pastors, Teachers, and even Apostles, and go all around the world and we never really learned how to be servants.

Jesus showed us an awesome example of serving in that He laid down His life for us. The ones that God will use the greatest for His kingdom will do the same. Matthew 20:26-28, "But it shall not be so among you; but whosoever will be great among you, let him be your minister; and whosoever will be chief among you, let him be your servant: Even as the Son of man came not to be ministered unto, but to minister, and to give his life a ransom for many." Apostle Paul and Apostle Peter said, "I, a servant of Jesus Christ and an Apostle"; they learned what it meant to serve others. Romans 1:1, II Peter 1:1. Elisha served Elijah and it was during this time that Elisha got trained up and God opened up the prophetic anointing so mightily for his life that he was able to see, hear, smell, taste, and feel things in the realm of the spirit. Remember, the anointing is tangible. We also need to notice how determined and persevering Prophet Elisha was in going for the things of God. In II Kings 2:1-6, Prophet Elijah tried to discourage Prophet Elisha to stay behind as he went on to Bethel, then again to Jericho, and a third time to Jordan. Each time, however, Prophet Elisha knew how to fight for his blessings, knowing that God had called him and not man, and he said in verses 2, 4, and 6, "As the Lord liveth and as thy soul liveth, I will not leave thee." This is how we need to be for the things of God!!! We need to learn to humble ourselves, cool down, settle down, set ourselves apart and learn the ways of Our God.

Every office has its' functions and responsibilities. However, they should all work together so smoothly like the wheels of the cherubims in book of Ezekiel 1:15-21 as they accomplished the things of the Lord. Everything worked so smoothly because they worked by the spirit as it says in verses 20 and 21. "Whithersoever the spirit was to go, they went, thither was their spirit to go; and the wheels were lifted up over against them: for the spirit of the living creature was in the wheels. When those went, these went; and when those stood, these stood; and when those were lifted up from the earth, the wheels were lifted up over against them: for the spirit of the living creature was in the wheels." However, in order for us to know our functions and responsibilities we must first know Our God. God the Father created us to praise, to glorify, and to magnify His name. He created us to serve Him. In the past He use to glorify and magnify Himself — Look throughout the Word — He says: "I am that I am," Exodus 3:14, "For I am the Lord thy God," the Holy one of Israel, thy Saviour," Isaiah 43:11, "Yea, before the day was I am he, and there is none that can deliver out of my hand: I will work, and who shall let it?" Isaiah 43:13, "I am the first, and I am the last; and beside me there is no God." Isaiah 44:6, and many, many more scriptures of God glorifying and magnifying Himself! The angels continually worship and glorify Him day and night. Then God the Father created us so that we too could worship and exalt His Holy Name. God the Father, Jehovah Jireh, is also the one who provides for us! Philippians 4:19, "But my God shall supply all your need according to his riches in glory by Christ Jesus." God the Father made the way for us by sending His only begotten son, Jesus Christ! Jesus, Our Lord and Saviour, came from heaven in the flesh to die for us, to open up the heavens for us, to reestablish the communications back between the Father and us. Jesus came to take all our sorrows, all our curses, and all our infirmities upon Himself, that we may have life and life more abundantly. Jesus, by becoming man, showed us how to live and walk in the spirit in this world; what a powerful, glorious, loving example Jesus was and is!!!

Jesus is the one who gives us our calling as the Word says that before He ascended He called some to be Apostles, Prophets, Evangelists, Pastors, and Teachers in Ephesians 4:8-11. Jesus said I am leaving but I am sending you The Comforter, the Holy Spirit. The Holy Spirit is the one who convicts us, brings us home, He guides us, and He cleanses us so that we can walk in Holiness. It is by the Holy Spirit that we receive deliverance for He is the finger of God. Luke 11:20; "But if I with the finger of God cast out devils, no doubt the Kingdom of God is come upon you." The Holy Spirit is the one who brings the Bride unto the Son, Jesus, in the clouds and Jesus presents us to the Father. (I Thessalonians 4:16, 17) The Holy Spirit is the one who enables us to operate in the 9 gifts of the Spirit according to I Corinthians 12:7-11. We also need to know the angels of the Lord and what their functions are and how they work for us. Not only do we need to know God the Father, God the Son, Jesus, and God, the Holy Spirit, and the angels of God, but we also need to know who our enemy is in order to know how to use our gifts and calling and to move in the power of God to destroy the enemies kingdom. (Luke 9:1) We will go more in depth of knowing the enemy and the tactics of the enemy in a later chapter. However, we need to know the enemy came to kill, steal and destroy and he hasn't changed, his tactics are the same.

The Apostles build the platform for the Prophets; who as the Word says, are secondarily in place. After Jesus Christ ascended into heaven, the Word of God says in Ephesians 4:11, 12, and 13, "And he gave some, apostles; and some, prophets; and some, evangelists; and some, pastors and teachers; for the perfecting of the saints, for the work of the ministry, for the edifying of the body of Christ: Till we all come in the unity of the faith, and of the knowledge of the Son of God, unto a perfect man, unto the measure of the stature of the fullness of Christ." Notice that as it says in Ephesians 4:8, 9, and 10, "Wherefore he saith, When he ascended up on high, he led captivity captive, and gave gifts unto men. (Now that he ascended, what is it but that he also descended first into the lower parts of the earth? He that descended is the same also that ascended up far above all heavens, that he might fill all things.") Each of us needs to know our gifts and calling and

how to operate in them by the Holy Spirit. God did not call u
in church for years and years and years; it should only take us th.
four years at the most to be trained up and sent out for the work o ...1e
Lord. We need to be producing fruit like the parable given by Jesus in
Luke 13:6-9, "He spake also this parable; A certain man had a fig tree
planted in his vineyard; and he came and sought fruit thereon, and
found none. Then said he unto the dresser of his vineyard, Behold,
these three years I come seeking fruit on this fig tree, and find none:
cut it down; why cumbereth it the ground? And he answering said
unto him, Lord, let it alone this year also, till I shall dig about it and
dung it: and if it bear fruit, well: and if not, then after that thou shalt
cut it down." If we are not yet producing fruit, ask the Lord to lead
you to a true five-fold ministry where He wants you to be so you can
step into the call that God has for you.

The Word of God is what separates the flesh from the spirit
according to Hebrews 4:12; so if we don't have the Word of God in
our lives richly, we are going to mix the soulish realm with the spirit.
This is why it is important for the Apostles to build the platform, so
that the prophetic word may be established. An example would be
that when a Prophet receives a prophetic word from the Lord, they
present it to the Apostle. The Apostle then chews on it to weigh it out
to see if first, it is from the Throne of God; then second to see if it is
God's timing to release it. If so, on both accounts, the Apostle releases
the prophetic word or allows the prophetic word to be spoken by the
Prophet. A good example of this is in the book of Acts 2:16-20 when
the Apostle Peter released the prophetic word that had been spoken
by the Prophet Joel; He said, "This is that which was spoken by the
Prophet Joel in the Word of God." (Joel 2:28)

Understanding each office or calling enables the body of Christ
(the church) to be built up and perfected in unity. We, the church, are
built up by receiving revelation upon revelation of who Jesus Christ is
for our lives and by this are we able to go from Glory to Glory. As He
spoke to his disciples in Matthew 16:13-19; when Jesus spoke, "He saith
unto them, But whom say ye that I am? And Simon Peter answered
and said, "Thou art the Christ, the Son of the living God. And Jesus
answered and said unto him, "Blessed art thou, Simon Barjona for
flesh and blood hath not revealed it unto thee, but my Father which
is in heaven. And I say also unto thee, that thou art Peter, and upon

this rock I will build my church; and the gates of hell shall not prevail against it." As of now, I see because we don't have the five-fold ministry in operation throughout the body of Christ, that the gates of hell are prevailing, the people of God are not blessed, and the church is not being built up ... (people are broke and in need, relationships are being broken, families are being destroyed and it seems like 3, 5, 10, even 20 years and the people of God are still suffering from the same problems, etc.) This is not what God wants for us!

See how the revelations come to the Apostles and Prophets; Apostle Peter moving in the realm of the spirit received the revelation from God the Father that Jesus Christ is the Son of the Living God and this revelation is the chief corner stone that the church is built upon. This revelation for the church, we the Gentiles, came to pass in the book of Acts 10 when Cornelius, a centurion, which the Word of God says, that he was a devout man, who feared God, and did many good works but Cornelius still needed to have the truth. The Truth is that we have to receive Jesus Christ as Our Lord and Saviour and follow Him, The Word of God, and have the five fold ministry and following the doctrines of the Apostles according to Acts 2:42 to enter the kingdom of Heaven. You see how Jesus was saying that upon the revelation that Jesus is the Christ, the Son of the living God that His church would be established; and the growth of the church is not building a bigger church building, growth comes when the revelations of who Jesus Christ, Our God, is for our lives and the revelations being imparted in us. Notice how Jesus said unto Peter "flesh and blood hath not revealed it unto thee but my Father which is in heaven."...It is the rhema word not the logos word that God establishes and builds His church. The rhema is the revelatory of the Word of God, whereas the logos word is just the written word of God. The rhema word brings life in you; like Apostle Paul said in Galatians 4:19, "My little children, of whom I travail in birth again until Christ be formed in you." It is through God the Father that we receive the Revelation of who His Son is for our lives so that we may worship Him in Spirit and Truth. Ephesians 3:1-5 explains that the revelations, the mysteries of the word of God are given unto His Holy Apostles and Prophets. "For this cause I Paul, the prisoner of Jesus Christ for you Gentiles, If ye have heard of the dispensation of the grace of God which is given me to you-ward: How that by revelation he made known unto me the mystery, (as I wrote afore in few words, Whereby, when ye read, ye may understand my knowledge in the mystery of Christ) Which in other ages was not made known unto the sons of men, as it is now revealed unto his holy apostles and prophets by the Spirit." (Notice the Word says Holy Apostles and Prophets; that means being separated for the Lord, seeking His face.)

The way you get to know someone is by their thoughts and their ways being revealed to you; the same with Our God. Without the true revelations of who He truly is, we cannot be like Him. I Corinthians 2:10, 11, "But God hath revealed them unto us by His Spirit for the Spirit searcheth all things, yea, the deep things of God. For what man knoweth the things of a man, save the spirit of man which is in him? Even so, the things of God knoweth no man but the Spirit of God." As the revelations of the Word of God come forward, so is He (JESUS) revealed to us and God can change us from Glory to Glory!!!

Again, I want to mention how many people try to negate that the Apostles and the Prophets are for today, but as you can see clearly according to the word of God these are given unto us after Jesus ascended on high. (Ephesians 4:8-13) It is not referring to the original twelve Apostles because the Word of God says that Jesus continues to give these gifts and callings after He ascended to heaven. Almost 1800 years ago they took the Apostles and the Prophets out of the church and when they did that they also took the spirit of holiness out of the church and this is why many people preach on prosperity and grace instead of repentance. Understand that the Holy Apostles and Prophets are the ones who are able to go into the hearts of the people to show them their transgressions so that repentance can come. The kingdom of God is all about repentance. Again, as you read in Ephesians 2:20 the foundations are built upon the Holy Apostles and Prophets, and it clearly tells us in Psalms 11:3, "If the foundations be destroyed, what can the righteous do?" An example of this is in Acts chapter 8:5-24, when God used the Evangelist Philip to preach the Gospel and Simon, formerly a sorcerer, accepted Jesus Christ as his Lord and Saviour and even got baptized in water. (Verses 12, 13) Simon still needed deliverance and Apostle Peter saw that Simon wanted to buy the power of God when he saw the Apostles laying hands on people and receiving the Holy Spirit. In verses 20 and 23, Apostle Peter said to Simon; "Thy money perish with thee....", "For I perceive that thou art in the gall of bitterness..." Through the Apostles and Prophets being able to see in

13

the hearts of God's people they can come clean with God, be delivered and established on the right foundations. It is only through having the Apostles and the Prophets that the apostolic (spiritual fathers) and the prophetic anointing is able to come forward that we can go into the hearts of the people that they can come clean with their God and walk in holiness separated unto Him. I Corinthians 14:25 says, "And thus are the secrets of his heart made manifest; and so falling down on his face he will worship God, and report that God is in you of a truth." If we are preaching on prosperity and not on repentance those riches are going to have wings like the word of God says in the book of Proverbs. Also, James 5:2 says, "Your riches are corrupted, and your garments are motheaten." Our focus needs to be on the Blesser, Jesus Christ, not on the blessings. And if we are preaching on the grace of God and not on repentance, it is because we are in sin and not coming clean with Our God. Like the Apostle Paul says in Romans 6:1, 2, "What shall we say then? Shall we continue in sin, that grace may abound? God forbid. How shall we, that are dead to sin, live any longer therein?" The grace of God is so that when we do make a mistake we can repent and come clean with our God; not so we can excuse ourselves to continue on with the same problem. We need to live by the grace of God and preach repentance just like my Jesus did. He gave understanding of His grace but He preached repentance, as in Matthew 4:17 He says, "From that time Jesus began to preach, and to say, Repent for the Kingdom of heaven is at hand."

When we truly understand Our God and reverence Him, the grace of God and riches and wealth will be in Our House that we will have no need. Psalms 112:1-3 says, "Praise ye the Lord. Blessed is the man that feareth the Lord, that delighteth greatly in his commandments. His seed shall be mighty upon earth: the generation of the upright shall be blessed. Wealth and riches shall be in his house; and his righteousness endureth for ever." We need to live for Him, serve Him, and stop living in sin, so the riches and wealth can come in; it is not by asking for money or by saying give me, give me, my name is Jimmy. The Prophets of God throughout the bible called everyone to repentance and the way to prepare our hearts for the Lord is Repentance. Jesus himself said, "Repent for the Kingdom of God is at hand." If we make a mistake, repent, get back up and go again.... for the word of God says in Hebrews 10:39, "But we are not of them who draw back unto perdition; but of them that believe to the saving of the soul." It is more important how we finish the race then how we start. Ecclesiastes 7:8, "Better is the end of a thing than the beginning thereof." The Apostles and Prophets are needed to bring back into the church the spirit of holiness. Repentance is the key to walking in Holiness. For those doubting Thomas's that need to see it with their eyes, let us read it in the Bible and notice the various Apostles called after Jesus ascended on high. Matthias in Acts 1:26, Barnabas and Paul in Acts 14:14, Andronicus and Junia in Romans 16:7, James, Jesus' brother in Galatians 1:19. I personally bless the Lord Jesus Christ for My Apostle, who God has used mightily to chastise me and bring correction into my life. Thank you, Jesus!!!

To know how powerfully the church is when we have the five fold ministry working together, let us look at I Samuel 17:40 when David went to go face the giant, Goliath.

I Samuel 17:40 says, "And he took his staff in his hand, and chose him five smooth stones out of the brook and put them in a shepherd's bag which he had,..." The staff in his hand represented the authority that God has given us to go against the works of the enemy and the five smooth stones represent the five-fold ministry in operation. David knew who his God was and is. David didn't measure things by what he saw or what he heard; he measured it by what he believed. David knew that if God is for us, who can be against us; so when he looked at Goliath and heard what he had to say he was not moved. Read what the Word says in I Samuel 17:44-46, "And the Philistine said to David, Come to me, and I will give thy flesh unto the fowls of the air, and to the beasts of the field. Then said David to the Philistine, Thou comest to me with a sword, and with a spear, and with a shield: but I come to thee in the name of the Lord of hosts, the God of the armies of Israel, whom thou hast defied. This day will the Lord deliver thee into mine hand; and I will smite thee, and take thine head from thee" and I will give the carcases of the host of the Philistines this day unto the fowls of the air, and to the wild beasts of the earth; that all the earth may know that there is a God in Israel." In order to kill the giants in our lives, we need the five-fold ministry working together. Remember what the Word of God says in I Corinthians 12:14-18; the foot can't be without the hand; the ear can't be without the eye, etc. We need to all work together for the church to be found without spot or wrinkle or any such thing according to Ephesians 5:27. Another example in the Word of God is in John 5:1-9 where it mentions about the pool of Bethesda. Notice in John 5:2 it specifies that the Pool of Bethesda had five porches; representing the five-fold ministry - notice the anointing was there for people to receive their healing. When we work together in unity in the five-fold ministry, the power of God is there to heal, deliver, and make free all that are in bondage. This is how the church is built; being fitly joined together into one body, which is Jesus Christ Our Lord and Saviour. That's what this is all about, that the body of Christ can be perfected and walking in unity.

Remember in the book of Genesis chapter 11:1-6 when the people were in unity to build a tower whose top could reach unto heaven, that God, Himself had to put a stop to it because they were trying to get to heaven their way and not God's way. What you need to notice though is the power God says there is in unity. Genesis 11:6 says, "And the Lord said, Behold, the people is one, and they have all one language, and this they begin to do: and now nothing will be restrained from them, which they have imagined to do." This time was a time of lawlessness and God said the thoughts and intents of man were wicked and He put a stop to it by confounding their language that they could not understand one another. (Genesis 11:7) Then God brought forth the law and people thought by their works that they could go into the heavens and found out this was impossible as well. Blessed be God the Father for sending His son, Jesus Christ, as Our Saviour. And Glory to the Lord Jesus Christ that after He ascended into heaven He sent His Holy Spirit. In the book of Acts Chapter 2:1-12 when Jesus sent forth the Baptism of the Holy Spirit and through the new tongue the pure language was brought forward by the Spirit of the Living God. This pure language was prophesied by the Prophet Zephaniah 3:9, "For then will I turn to the people a pure language that they may all call upon the name of the Lord, to serve him with one consent." By His Spirit are we able to come into a true unity; working together for the perfection of the body of Christ. Unity only comes by us being one in His Spirit. Psalm 133:1, 2, "Behold how good and how pleasant it is for brethren to dwell together in unity! It is like the precious ointment upon the head, that ran down upon the beard, even Aaron's beard: that went down to the skirts of his garments." Notice the anointing is thru the Prophet. Aaron was a Prophet and a Prophet brings the anointing into the church.

Many of us know how Apostle Peter had told Jesus that though everyone else may get offended by Him that he himself would not and Jesus told Peter that before the cock crows that Peter would deny Him thrice. Read Matthew 26:33, 34. Just as Jesus had told this to Peter so it happened. Matthew 26:75, "And Peter remembered the word of Jesus, which said unto him, "Before the cock crow, thou shalt deny me thrice. And he went out, and wept bitterly." Many believe that this is why in the Book of John 21:15-18 that because Peter had denied Jesus three times that this is why Our Lord Jesus asked Peter three times if he loved Him. This is good and this is true however, let's go even deeper, understanding the revelation of those scriptures. Verse 15, "So when they had dined Jesus saith to Simon Peter, "Simon, son of Jonas, lovest thou me more than these:" He saith unto him, "Yea, Lord thou knowest that I love thee." He saith unto him, "Feed my lambs." He saith to him again the second time, "Simon, son of Jonas, lovest thou me?" He saith unto him, "Yea, Lord; thou knowest that I love thee." He saith unto him, "Feed my sheep." He saith unto him the third time, "Simon, son of Jonas, lovest thou me?" Peter was grieved because he said unto him the third time, "Lovest thou me?" And he said unto him, "Lord, thou knowest all things; thou knowest that I love thee." Jesus saith unto him, "Feed my sheep. Verily, verily, I say unto thee, when thou wast young, thou girdesdst thyself, and walkedst whither thou wouldest: but when thou shalt be old, thou shalt stretch forth thy hands, and another shall gird thee, and carry thee whither thou wouldest not." See, first Jesus was asking Peter if he loved him more than the other apostles and the people around him. Second, Jesus was saying that if you truly love me, you will love your neighbor as yourself; you will even love your enemies. Thirdly, Jesus was saying that Peter had to love Jesus more than himself and that the only way Peter or any of us can have that Agape love (unconditional love) is through the Holy Spirit and by having the Holy Spirit within us we are able to lay down our lives for others. That is why Jesus told Peter and the disciples all to go wait for the promise and receive power, the Baptism of the Holy Spirit. Acts 1:4-8 shows us in having the Holy Spirit within us we can have oneness, that unity and agape love that is needed.

Here is an analogy of how the five-fold ministry (Apostles, Prophets, Evangelists, Pastors, and Teachers) can work together. There was an Evangelist and he was out on the streets telling everyone about the Gospel of Jesus Christ; that Jesus Christ loves us and has demonstrated that for us. There leaning up against a building was a young man who was drunk who overheard the Evangelist speaking the Word of the Lord and telling people they need to repent and give their hearts to Jesus Christ. The young man said, "I need that, I need that in my life," and he accepted Jesus Christ into his heart. That evening the Evangelist brought the young man to gather together with the other saints. When the Pastor saw the young man he said, "I see this young man needs a lot of lovin'." Then the Teacher standing right next to the Pastor said, "Well that is very true, that he needs a lot of Loving, but I also see that he needs the Word of God broken down and simplified that he can apply it to his everyday life." Then up walked the Prophet and said, "Yes, this man needs to know he is loved, he needs the Word of God in his life but what the Lord is showing me in his heart is that he was rejected by his father and he has a spirit of bondage and addiction in him." Then standing right next to the Prophet, of course, is the Apostle, who says, "That is right, he not only needs the loving, to be taught the Word of God, he needs to be delivered, made free and baptized with the Holy Ghost, and stir up the gifting within him that he too can live as God called him to live fulfilling the call of God in his life." There we have it the five-fold ministry working together.

Jesus Christ, Our Lord and Saviour fulfilled all five offices while He was here on earth that He would show us how. As mentioned before, according to Hebrews 3:1, Jesus was and is the first Apostle; He came to activate the gifts and callings in His Apostles' and the dicsciples' lives. Jesus is The Prophet; as in John 4:5-42, when the woman of Samaria came to the well He told her everything that she ever did; He knew peoples' thoughts, He knew the past, the present, and the future, the only thing Jesus said that Only the Father knows is when heaven and earth shall pass away. (Matthew 24:35, 36) Jesus was an Evangelist drawing thousands unto Himself and preaching of the kingdom of God, moving in signs and wonders. Matthew 9:35, "And Jesus went about all the cities and villages, teaching in their synagogues, and preaching the gospel of the kingdom, and healing every sickness and every disease among the people." Such great multitudes were drawn to Him that He even used the water to be a megaphone for Him so that all could hear the Good News. (Mark 4:1) Jesus is Our Pastor as the Word of God says in Psalms 23; watching over us as Our Shepherd as spoken in I Peter 2:25, "For ye were as sheep going astray; but are now returned unto the Shepherd and Bishop of your souls." Jesus as the Teacher spoke it by the Spirit; they referred to Him as Rabbi because they recognized the Word in Him. (John 3:2) Like the Apostle Peter said to Jesus, "Lord to whom shall we go? Thou hast the words of eternal life." When Jesus taught that we need to eat his body and drink his blood, the teaching was too hard for the people that wanted to do it their way and so they left and Jesus asked the disciples, "Will ye also go away?" (John 6:53:69) Jesus was The Apostle, The Prophet, The Evangelist, The Pastor, and The Teacher as He walked here on the earth. He is All in All!!

Now we will go into the different callings and understand more in depth how each calling functions so we can fulfill what God has for each of us. (Ephesians 4:11, 12, 13)

Pastors

Pastors, as we all know, are shepherds called to watch over the flock. Pastors are called to love and nurture God's people. Like the Word of God says in Psalms 23:1, "The Lord is my shepherd; I shall not want. So, a Pastor is called to tend to the sheep, which means that we need to be available. Setting up an appointment to see your Pastor in two to three weeks when you are in the midst of something is not of God....if we can't be there for someone we need to make sure that someone is available. A Pastor has a local vision because the calling of the office is to watch over their sheep. Jesus is the Good Shepherd in Matthew 15:29-32; He had compassion on the multitude knowing that if He would have sent them away hungry they would have fainted in the way. Read verse 32, "Then Jesus called his disciples unto him, and said, I have compassion on the multitude, because they continue with me now three days, and have nothing to eat: and I will not send them away fasting, lest they faint in the way." That is what a shepherd does; he tends to the sheep, he feeds the sheep, he is there to comfort the sheep and to lead them. I heard a funny story about two men that were deep sea fishing and their boat broke down and got stranded on an island. The one man was very upset and nervous and the other man was very calm saying, "Don't worry; don't worry." One day went by, two days went by and on the third day the one man that was very upset and nervous started getting angry with his friend and said, "I don't know how you can stay so calm when we are stranded out here on this island." His friend answered him, "You have to understand, I give $5000.00 a month in tithes and I know my pastor will be looking for me." (Hah, this is just to add a little humor here). The pastors are typically full of love, mercy and compassion making sure that his sheep are cared for. When I took a trip to Israel many years ago we were on a bus touring all of Israel as we passed one open field there were a lot of sheep and a man behind them poking the sheep with his staff. One of the people on the bus said, "Look at the shepherd and his sheep." The tour guide said, "That is not a shepherd; that is a shearer. He said you will always be able tell the difference because a shepherd is in the front leading and guiding to safety; whereas, a shearer is in the back prodding and driving the sheep to the slaughter." The same for our lives; Our Lord Jesus by His Spirit leads and guides us unlike the enemy which drives us to do things. Being a Pastor is a great responsibility of which we cannot take lightly. God gives warning to the Pastors that don't take care of and watch out for their flock. He says in His Word He will take them out and put others in that will take care of the flock. Let's read; Jeremiah 23:1-5, "Woe be unto the pastors that destroy and scatter the sheep of my pasture: saith the Lord. Therefore thus saith the Lord God of Israel against the pastors that feed my people; ye have scattered my flock, and driven them away, and have not visited them: behold, I will visit upon you the evil of your doings, saith the Lord. And I will gather the remnant of my flock out of all countries whither I have driven them, and will bring them again to their fold; and they shall be fruitful and increase. And I will set up shepherds over them which shall feed them: and they shall fear no more, nor be dismayed, neither shall they be lacking, saith the Lord." Jehovah God, through His Word is giving us Pastors warning to make sure we are watching out for His flock. This is why it is of utmost importance that we as Pastors are under the five-fold ministry that the work of the Lord does not become overbearing. Before we understood the importance of the five-fold ministry, we saw and experienced how the need of the people can be very pulling and demanding. However, being a Pastor under the five fold allows us to not be so pulled that we ourselves are lacking in that one on one relationship with Our God, Jesus Christ. Throughout the Old Testament the Prophets, Pastors, Evangelist, and Teachers were not able to bring the Body of Christ into unity. In Fact the Word of God says they hardly even had time with the Lord and God's people were famished for the Word. Jeremiah 10:21, "For the Pastors are become brutish, and have not sought the Lord: therefore they shall not prosper, and all their flocks shall be scattered."

When God told the Prophet Samuel, in I Samuel 16, to go anoint one of Jesse's sons to be king over Israel, you will notice that David was being a pastor out taking care of the sheep. I Samuel 16:11 says, "And Samuel said unto Jesse, Are here all thy children? And he said, There remaineth yet the youngest, and behold, he keepeth the sheep." David, unlike his brothers, wasn't sitting around in the house and doing nothing. David was tending to the sheep. In other words, if we have been in church for 5, 10, 15 years and we still haven't stepped into the call of God for our lives and watching and looking out for our brothers and sisters in Christ, something is wrong. God took notice of David because he was doing what he was suppose to be doing; caring for the sheep. David understood the importance of watching over the sheep, checking up on them and making sure they weren't being destroyed by the lions and bears. When Cain, Adam and Eve's son, said in Genesis 4:9, "Am I my brothers' keeper?", it was because Cain had unforgiveness, bitterness, and resentment in his heart that he did not want to look out for anyone else. The Word of God says we are to love our neighbors as ourselves. As Pastors we need to nurture, tend, feed, comfort, lead, protect, guide, guard, and have compassion on God's people. That's why a Pastor is called a Shepherd because they watch over the flock. The Pastors have the ability to impart into the believer a love for God's people.

Teachers

Teachers are set in the Body of Christ to teach, instruct, and expound on the Word of God. A teacher is able to break down and simplify the Word of God so that people are able to apply it to their everyday lives. All parents should be Teachers of the Word of God to their children. That is why the Bible tells us in Proverbs 22:6, "Train up a child in the way he should go: and when he is old, he will not depart from it." A Teacher needs to be mature and a good example; otherwise, we are just being hypocrites. James 3:1, 2, "My brethren, be not many masters, knowing that we shall receive the greater condemnation. For in many things we offend all. If any man offend not in word, the same is a perfect man and able also to bridle the whole body." A Teacher is able to disciple and to educate God's people which is very important because the bible says in Isaiah 5:13, "Therefore, my people are gone into captivity (bondage) because they have no knowledge." As if this is not bad enough to be in captivity, look what else the Prophet Hosea says in Hosea 4:6, "My people are destroyed for lack of knowledge." So, as you can see the calling of a Teacher is a very vital and important office for the training up of God's people.

A Teacher is able to explain the Word of God in such a way that through the Spirit of the Living God they are able to give God's people the keys they need to worship God in Spirit and in Truth! We need to realize being an awesome Teacher of the Word of God has nothing to do with age it has to do with us being full of the Word of God. Let's look at an example in the book of Luke chapter 2 when Jesus at 12 years old, he stayed behind in Jerusalem and was teaching the scribes and doctors. Luke 2:46, 47, "And it came to pass, that after three days they found him in the temple, sitting in the midst of the doctors, both hearing them, and asking them questions. And all that heard him were astonished at his understanding and answers." The Bible is very clear that he who God sends is full of the Word of God. John 3:34, "For he whom God hath sent speaketh the words of God: for God giveth not the Spirit by measure unto him." Notice what the Word of God is saying here in this scripture that if we are truly full of the Spirit of the Living God, all we will want to do is talk about Jesus, the Word of God. We need to be so full of the Word of God, for God's glory, that people are sitting down wanting to hear the revelations of the Word of God that God has given us. In Hebrews 4:12 the Bible says that the Word of God is quick and powerful, sharper than any two edged sword….Our sword should be so sharp that when anyone comes near us they get cut. In other words their spirit be quickened that the Word of God will cut away the flesh and enable them to walk this life in the spirit. Teachers should be able to explain and train up, to instruct and educate, to disciple and tutor God's people so that all may become mature in the ways of Our God, Jesus Christ. For each office God gives a special grace as the Word of God says in Ephesians 4:7, "But unto every one of us is given grace according to the measure of the Gift of Christ." God the Father gives a unique grace on the office of a Teacher that they will be able to help others grow in maturity. When the Word of God tells us to be perfect it is referring to being mature. Matthew 5:48, "Be ye therefore perfect; even as your Father which is in heaven is perfect."

We need to look at another awesome Teacher of the Word of God; the Apostle Paul, even though he was an Apostle, we need to understand that the Apostles are able to move in all five offices so that they can impart, instruct and train up God's people in every office. Apostle Paul loved teaching the Word of God so much that on one day it says in the Word of God that he was teaching all day and all night until the break of day. Acts 20:7-12, "And upon the first day of the week, when the disciples came together to break bread, Paul preached unto them, ready to depart on the morrow; and continued his speech until midnight. And there were many lights in the upper chamber, where they were gathered together. And there sat in a window a certain young man named Eutychus, being fallen into a deep sleep: and as Paul was long preaching, he sunk down with sleep, and fell down from the third loft, and was taken up dead. And Paul went down, and fell on him, and embracing him said, Trouble not yourselves: for his life is in him. When he therefore was come up again, and had broken bread, and eaten, and talked a long while, even till break of day, so he departed. And they brought the young man alive, and were not a little comforted." (I guess you could say that is another way of laying down your life for the Gospel of Jesus Christ. Chuckle, Chuckle!) I believe that even though the young man was very tired, he was hungry for the Word of God and didn't want to miss anything; that is why I believe God Almighty saw that hunger and when the Apostle Paul embraced him, God revived Eutychus' spirit. I know for myself, like many others, it's not just having the scriptures memorized - No, we need to have the revelations of what the Word of God is saying and we can only get that through the holy Apostles and Prophets by the Spirit. (Ephesians 3:1-5) An example of that is in Acts 18:24-27, where it talks about Apollos, the Word says that Apollos was an eloquent man, and mighty in the scriptures; however, at the time Aquila and Priscilla met him he only understood the Baptism of John and not the fullness of the revelations of the Word of God and the need for the five-fold ministry and the Baptism of the Holy Spirit. Aquila and Priscilla were awesome Teachers of the Word of God expounding and breaking it down so that Apollos could see the more perfect way. It made Apollos hungry for the things of God that when he met up with the Apostle Paul he was filled with the Holy Ghost, speaking in tongues, and began to prophesy. Read in Acts chapter 19:1-6. Also in Acts 19:7-10 the Apostle Paul had gone into Ephesus and when he saw the people that were hungry for the things of God, he continued with them for 2 years training them up and teaching them the ways of God. As a Teacher of the Word of God, that's how we should be scouting out and looking for those that have that hunger and passion and want to be taught and trained up in the ways of God. Some people only want to argue the Word of God; that is a religious spirit and don't waste your time. II Timothy 2:14 says, "Of these things put them in remembrance, charging them before the Lord that they strive not about words to no profit, but to the subverting of the hearers." For those that do want the revelations and hunger for the Word of God remember what Jesus said in Matthew 5:6, "Blessed are they which do hunger and thirst after righteousness: for they shall be filled." A Teacher of the Word of God is able to simplify the Word so that it taste like honey and fresh bread as it goes in because it is the revelations of the Word of God. "O Taste and see that the Lord is good: blessed is the man that trusteth in him." Psalm 34:8.

Evangelists

Evangelists are a powerful part of the five-fold ministry. Evangelists are after the souls; and if we know the heart of Our God, It Is Souls. The Bible says in II Peter 3:9, "The Lord is not slack concerning his promise, as some men count slackness; but is longsuffering to us-ward, not willing that any should perish, but that all should come to repentance." An Evangelists main purpose is to tell people the Good News. One of the most powerful Evangelists mentioned in the Bible is in John chapter 4, the Samaritan woman at the well. When Jesus revealed all the secrets in her heart, she accepted Jesus Christ as the True Messiah. (Verses 17-26) Immediately, the woman left and told everyone in the city about Jesus and won many of the people of the city over for Jesus. John 4:28-30, "The woman then left her waterpot, and went her way into the city, and saith to the men, Come, see a man, which told me all things that ever I did: is not this the Christ? Then they went out of the city and came unto him." John 4:39, "And many of the Samaritans of that city believed on him for the saying of the woman which testified, He told me all that ever I did."

An Evangelist moves in signs and wonders to demonstrate the Power of God. Like the Apostle Paul, moving in the Evangelistic, says in I Corinthians 2:4, "And my speech and my preaching was not with enticing words of man's wisdom, but in demonstration of the Spirit and of Power." People need to know Our God, Jesus Christ, is a living God and by His Power are we saved, healed, and delivered. Glory to God, forever! The five-fold ministry needs Evangelists that want to be out there doing the work of the Lord, telling people the Gospel and compelling them to come. Another example of two awesome Evangelists are in the book of Acts 6:1-15 and Acts 8:5-7. The Apostles were very busy and they knew they needed help in the ministration of the daily needs of the people so they said in Acts 6:3, "Wherefore, brethren, look ye out among you seven men of honest report, full of the Holy Ghost and wisdom whom we may appoint over this business." Stephen and Philip were among those seven men and they did serve the needs of the people, but they also knew the importance of stepping into their calls as Evangelists, under the Apostolic, and telling people the Good News. Reading Acts chapters 6-9, I believe because of Stephen preaching the Gospel and being such an awesome example that God used him to plant the seed in the Apostle Paul's life. Even while they were stoning Stephen to death as the Word of God says in Acts 7:58-60, he continued to preach the good news. Let's read it: "And cast him out of the city, and stoned him: and the witnesses laid down their clothes at a young man's feet, whose name was Saul (Who later became known as Apostle Paul). And they stoned Stephen, calling upon God, and saying, Lord Jesus, receive my spirit. And he kneeled down, and cried with a loud voice, "Lord, lay not this sin to their charge. And when he had said this, he fell asleep." Remember, some plant, and some water, but God reaps the harvest. That is what Apostle Paul said in I Corinthians 3:6, "I have planted, Apollos watered; but God gave the increase." Then there was Philip who moved in signs and wonders. Read Acts 8:5-7, "Then Philip went down to the city of Samaria, and preached Christ unto them. And the people with one accord gave heed unto those things which Philip spake, hearing and seeing the miracles which he did. For unclean spirits, crying with loud voice, came out of many that were possessed with them; and many taken with palsies, and that were lame, were healed." Philip was walking in the spirit so mightily that after he preached the gospel and baptized the Ethiopian Eunuch in Acts 8:26-40, that the Spirit of the Living God transported him to where he needed to be next. Now, that's better than owning your own jet airplane!! Glory to the Lord, forever! As you can see, Philip and Stephen wanted the things of God and for Jesus Christ to be glorified through their lives so they went about telling others about the Good News.

Two-thirds of the name of GOD is GO. This is the Great Commission Jesus spoke to all the disciples before He ascended into heaven. Matthew 28:19, "Go ye therefore, and teach all nations, baptizing them in the name of the Father, and of the Son, and of the Holy Ghost." We need to understand also that Our God is a God of Order; God is not going to send us to China or Central America or some other foreign country if we are not trained up, activated, and spreading the Good News in our own areas. The Word of God says in Acts 1:8, "....and ye shall be witnesses unto me both in Jerusalem, and in all Judaea, and in Samaria, and unto the uttermost part of the earth." This means we need to be good examples in our homes and at our jobs and we need to be telling people about Jesus in our local area and then God will send us out to the nations. Many people say they want to go on a mission trip to Central America or China and their neighbors don't even know they serve Jesus because they are ashamed of the Gospel. We need to all be sharing the Good News even if our calling is not that of an Evangelist. Remember what the Apostle Paul says about the Power of God, that it is in preaching the gospel. I Corinthians 1:18; "For the preaching of the cross is to them that perish foolishness; but unto us which are saved it is the power of God."

The Good News should be like fire shut up in our bones (Jeremiah 20:9); where we are compelled to share. This is how it was for four leprous men in II Kings 7:1-9. There was a great famine in Samaria at that time and the four leprous men went into the camp of the Syrians to see what they could find. I believe the great famine represented the lack of the Word of God being read or spoken. The Lord Himself, working behind the scenes, had scattered the enemy so that those that were willing to lose their lives would save their lives. Just like these leprous men, we need to realize God is working behind the scenes for us. This was the case with the four leprous men and when they found all the spoils of the Syrians, they couldn't help but go back and share the Good News with all the others. II Kings 7:9; "Then they said one to another, We do not well: this day is a day of Good Tidings, and we hold our peace; if we tarry till the morning light, some mischief will come upon us now therefore come, that we may go and tell the king's household." We all need to be like that; winning souls for the Lord. Knowing that we have found the Precious Pearl we need to be so excited that we want everyone to know. As an Evangelist, when someone is ready to become born again, we need to be ready to lead them according to the Word of God into the kingdom as it says in Romans 10:9, "That if thou shalt confess with thy mouth the Lord Jesus, and shalt believe in thine heart that God hath raised him from the dead, thou shalt be saved."

Here it is in prayer form for the person or persons to repeat after you:

"Lord Jesus, come into my heart, I confess that I am a sinner and I have sinned against your Holy Name. Forgive me Lord, cleanse me and wash me with your blood. I confess with my mouth that Jesus Christ is my Lord and my Saviour, and I believe in my heart that God the Father raised Jesus from the dead. I thank you, Father, for putting my name in the Lambs book of Life." Now say, "satan, you are not my God, Jesus Christ is my God and I renounce everything that has to do with you. And I forgive from my heart everyone who ever hurt me or went against me; and Father God, Lord Jesus I ask you to forgive me for everyone I have hurt and just as important, I forgive myself." (It is very important that we forgive ourselves. Romans 8:1, "There is therefore now no comdemnation to them which are in Christ Jesus, who walk not after the flesh, but after the Spirit.")

An Evangelist goes out looking for the lost, shares the Good News, showing people the way unto salvation. Like the Word of God says in Proverbs 11:30, "The fruit of the righteous is a tree of life; and he that winneth souls is wise." So let us go, Evangelize, Evangelize, Evangelize!!!

Prophets

If you ask most people, "What is a Prophet?" they will tell you a Prophet is the mouthpiece of God. This is true, Prophets are the mouthpiece of God; they are like a trumpet as it says in Isaiah 58:1, "Cry aloud, spare not, lift up thy voice like a trumpet, and shew my people their transgression, and the house of Jacob their sins." To think, Our God, Our Creator, Our Lord and King, Jesus Christ would choose to use us as His mouthpiece and enable us to have that intimacy with Him that He begins revealing the secret things unto us. Wow! There is so much more for us in understanding what a Prophet is and how God uses them.

The Prophetic is so awesome, exciting, powerful, and adventurous. Now looking at the Prophetic we need to visualize it or have a picture in our minds so that we can have a better understanding. You see the Prophetic is like a swimming pool; there is the shallow end, the middle part and the deep end. The shallow part of the pool is not the office of a Prophet it is the prophetic gifting as mentioned in I Corinthians 12:10; the gift of prophecy is one of the nine gifts of the Spirit. The gift of prophecy is described in I Corinthians 14:3, "But he that prophesieth speaketh unto men to edification, and exhortation, and comfort." Knowing that even a little child can swim in the shallow end of the pool with floaties and/or with proper supervision; so it is with the prophetic gift. Prophets and everyone in a five-fold ministry can be used in the gift of prophecy but it needs to be in order. The Apostle Paul says in the Word in I Corinthians 14:39, "Wherefore, brethren, covet to prophesy, and forbid not to speak with tongues." I believe this is so needed in the Body of Christ because the Word says that in the last days many hearts are going to wax cold. When you're moving in the awesomeness of the prophetic, God will bring forth those words of prophesy by revelation which directly speaks to the hearts and draws God's people back to Him or enables someone to even have a closer relationship with the Lord. All Glory to the Lord!

Now, we start getting into the middle part of the swimming pool; this represents the Office of a Prophet. Not many people want to enter in; why, because we need to be willing to lose it all to gain it all. A Prophet of God needs to be separated, set apart loving on the Lord, worshipping the Lord, ministering unto the Lord and having that passion and hunger for the Word of God. Job said it like this, "Neither have I gone back from the commandment of his lips, I have esteemed the words of his mouth more than my necessary food." (Job 23:12) A Prophet is like an eagle because as you know eagles soar high and they soar alone; they don't fly in flocks. In other words we as Prophets of God need to be separated and in the presence of Our Almighty God that we are able to hear His Voice all the time. As the Word of God says in Isaiah 40:31; "But they that wait upon the Lord shall renew their strength; they shall mount up with wings as eagles; they shall run, and not be weary; and they shall walk, and not faint." When we are like the eagles we don't grow weary ministering unto the Lord, seeking His face; that's the waiting on the Lord it is referring to; similar to a waitress or waiter. When we are in the presence of Our God worshipping Him, He inhales our worship unto Himself as a sweet aroma and He exhales, breathes out, revelation upon revelation to the Prophet as the Word says in Ephesians 3:1-5 that the mysteries, the revelations are given to the Holy Apostles and Prophets.

Prophets are like eagles also because they are known for their excellent eyesight; it is known that an eagle has two foveae or centers of focus, that allow them to see both forward and to the side at the same time. This is how we have to be as Prophets of God, knowing what's going on around us at all times. It's like a negotiator when he goes in he scans the whole scene, knowing everything that is going on; same for a Prophet of God walking in the spirit is able to see, hear, smell, taste, and even feel what is going on in the realm of the spirit. Also, an eagle's eyesight is so powerful they are able to see 8 miles ahead (8 meaning new beginnings); the same for a Prophet seeing the new beginnings God has for that man or woman of God, or for a congregation or even for a whole nation. Psalm 91:1 says, "He that dwelleth in the secret place of the most High shall abide under the shadow of the Almighty." A Prophet should be in that secret place with the Lord where they can see peoples' past so that they may be delivered, their present so they can see where they are in their walk with the Lord and the gifts and calling of God in their lives and their future so that they can see the plans God has for them for a future and a hope as spoken by the Prophet Jeremiah. Jeremiah 29:11 says, "For I know the thoughts that I think toward you, saith the Lord, thoughts of peace, and not of evil, to give you an expected end." An eagle has two eyelids; the inner eyelid slides across the eye every three to four seconds wiping away any dirt or dust and because this inner eyelid is translucent even while it is clearing any debris the eagle can still see through it. Having this keen eyesight enables the eagle to see and take its' prey alive; the same way a Prophet of God living in the spirit is able to discern even the most hidden secret in order to destroy the works of the devil just like Jesus came to do. I John 3:8, "...For this purpose, the Son of God was manifested, that he might destroy the works of the devil." This is why a Prophet in the middle part of the pool needs to be walking in the anointing because without the anointing we cannot help anyone to get out of bondage. For the anointing is the Burden Removing, Yoke Destroying, POWER OF GOD! Isaiah 10:27, "And it shall come to pass in that day, that his burden shall be taken away from off thy shoulder, and his yoke from off thy neck, and the yoke shall be destroyed because of the anointing." By having the anointing we can destroy every yoke of bondage by casting out all that is not of the Lord in a person's life. I once heard someone say, "You can tell the anointing a person carries by the scars he/she bore." In other words, when the flesh gets cut away by the Word of God thru the trials we go through, then God puts that anointing in us to help others. I Peter 4:1, 2, "Forasmuch then as Christ hath suffered for us in the flesh, arm yourselves likewise with the same mind: for he that hath suffered in the flesh hath ceased from sin; that he no longer should live the rest of his time in the flesh to the lust of men, but to the will of God." The anointing makes a way, opens doors, for the man or woman of God. Proverbs 18:16, "A man's gift maketh room for him, and bringeth him before great men." A Prophet carrying and walking in the anointing changes the atmosphere because they bring in the presence of God. Many people only want the Prophets to come and bring them a good word from the Lord, but what would a good word do for you if you have bitterness or unforgiveness or some other form of sin and your salvation is at stake. That is why God gives a strong word of warning to the Prophets that only give good words and don't reveal the secrets of people's hearts that they can be delivered and going to heaven. Lamentations 2:14, "Thy prophets have seen vain and foolish things for thee: and they have not discovered thine iniquity, to turn away thy captivity; but have seen for thee false burdens and causes of banishment." A Prophet, like an eagle is able to see into the deep obscure places even into the very hearts of people.

Like the Word of God says in I Corinthians 14:25, "And thus are the secrets of his heart made manifest; and so falling down on his face he will worship God, and report that God is in you of a truth." This is why we as Prophets of God need to be separated, walking in Holiness unto the Lord so that when we go into a person's heart we are able to take the splinter out because we have already taken the plank out of our own life. Remember, Matthew 7:3, 4, 5, "And why beholdest thou the mote that is in thy brother's eye, but considerest not the beam that is in thine own eye? Or how wilt thou say to thy brother, Let me pull out the mote out of thine eye; and, behold, a beam is in thine own eye? Thou hypocrite, First Cast out the beam out of thine own eye; and then shalt thou see clearly to cast out the mote out of thy brother's eye." Once we get the beam out of our own eye we will be walking with the love of the Lord Jesus to help others; sometimes that splinter in our brother or sister's life is the key that has been keeping them in bondage for so many years.

A Prophet in the middle part of the pool should be like the Prophets in the Old Testament which were judges discerning good and evil in order to help the people of God. We are called to be watchmen not watchdogs; watchdogs just bark (Grumble, complain, and find fault.), but don't move in the anointing to help anyone. Ezekiel 3:17 says, "Son of man, I have made thee a watchman unto the house of Israel: therefore hear the word at my mouth and give them warning from me." A watchman is like a gatekeeper keeping watch of what is approaching; that means the good and the bad such as, words of encouragement and discernment of what is not of the Lord. When we Prophets stand in our positions keeping watch, I believe the gates of Hell will not prevail. The Prophets are the ones who bring the anointing into the church; this is of utmost importance. John the Baptist was that Prophet who ushered in the Anointed One, Jesus. "The voice of one crying in the wilderness, "Prepare ye the way of the Lord, make His paths straight." (Matthew 3:13) Prophet Samuel in I Samuel 10:1 anointed Saul to be king over Israel; and then again he anointed David in I Samuel 16:13 to be king over Israel in place of Saul. The Prophets draw people to repentance and that is what God is looking for, a broken and contrite heart, recognizing that we need Our God. Prophets need to move and see in the realm of the spirit in order to become good intercessors for the Lord. Prophet Daniel and Prophet Ezra are good examples of Prophets moving as intercessors for God's people. Prophet Ezra in Ezra chapter 9 and Prophet Daniel in Daniel chapter 9 understood the importance of repentance; but if you read those chapters clearly you will see that even before they began to repent for themselves and for God's people, they entered into His presence with praise.

A Prophet needs to speak it just like it was given from the Lord, no watering down the Word of God. We need to stand like the Prophet Micaiah stood in I Kings 22:1-28. King Ahab, the king of Israel, and King Jehoshaphat, the king of Judah, were together and King Ahab wanted to go up to Ramoth-Gilead to take the land and he asked King Jehoshaphat to join him. King Jehoshaphat said in verse 5 let us inquire of the Lord. So, King Ahab asked 400 prophets in verse 6 and because they had a people pleasing spirit they told the King Ahab what he wanted to hear. The 400 prophets said in verse 6, "Go up; for the Lord shall deliver it into the hand of the king." But not Micaiah, he spoke as a true Prophet of God. Prophet Micaiah knew that when a person has an idol in their heart, that God answers them according to the idol in their heart. Notice in verse 15 of I Kings chapter 22, Prophet Micaiah answered King Ahab according to the idols in his heart first; like the Word of God shows us in Ezekiel 14:1-4 which says, "Then came certain of the elders of Israel unto me, and sat before me. And the word of the Lord came unto me saying, Son of man, these men have set up their idols in their heart, and put the stumbling block of their iniquity before their face: should I be inquired of at all by them? Therefore speak unto them, and say unto them, Thus saith the Lord God; Every man of the house of Israel that setteth up his idols in his heart, and putteth the stumbling block of his iniquity before his face, and cometh to the prophet; I the Lord will answer him that cometh according to the multitude of his idols." Then in verses 16-26 Prophet Micaiah told King Ahab exactly how it was and what the Lord was saying and what was going on in the realm of the spirit. (Notice in verse 21, 22, and 23, how the demonic spirits have to go to God first and get permission before they can come against anyone.) "And there came forth a spirit and stood before the Lord, and said, I will persuade him. And the Lord said unto him, "Wherewith?" And he said, I will go forth, and I will be a lying spirit in the mouth of all his prophets. And he said, "Thou shalt persuade him, and prevail also: go forth, and do so. Now therefore, behold, the Lord hath put a lying spirit in the mouth of all these thy prophets, and the Lord hath spoken evil concerning thee." This example in the Word of God is why it is so important when we are reading the Word of God we read it in the spirit and understand the revelations of the Word. We as Prophets of God need to stand on God's Word not compromising no matter how many other people stand with us. We need to say what the Lord has to say no matter the cost; remember this was two kings that Prophet Micaiah was speaking to but the Prophet feared God not man. The Word of God shows us clearly we are not here to please man; we are here to please God. Luke 6:26 says; "Woe unto you, when all men shall speak well of you! For so did their fathers to the false prophets." We are not here to make friends; we are here to speak the Word of the Lord that their souls should be saved and going to heaven.

A Prophet of God should be able to be in the spirit at any time; let's look in the book of Revelation 4:1, 2, "After this I looked, and behold a door was opened in heaven: and the first voice which I heard was as it were of a trumpet talking with me which said, "Come up hither, and I will shew thee things which must be hereafter. And immediately I was in the spirit: and behold a throne was set in heaven, and one sat on the throne." I want you to notice how the Word of God says that John was immediately in the spirit and could see in the realm of the spirit. The Lord used Apostle John powerfully in the prophetic that by the inspiration of the Holy Spirit, he wrote the book of Revelation. The other thing I want us to notice here is how the prophetic word, the book of Revelation, written by John has not been fulfilled yet; neither have all prophesies in the book of Daniel and Isaiah and others. The reason I am bringing this to light right now is because many of us are so quick to call or label someone a false Prophet when a prophecy has not yet been fulfilled. We need to understand by the Word of God what a false Prophet is: Acts 13:6, 7, 8, "And when they had gone through the isle unto Paphos, they found a certain sorcerer, a false prophet, a Jew, whose name was Barjesus: which was with the deputy of the country, Sergius Paulus, a prudent man; who called for Barnabas and Saul, and desired to hear the word of God. But Elymas, the sorcerer (for so is his name by interpretation) withstood them, seeking to turn away the deputy from the faith." A false Prophet as you see is someone who turns people away from the truth, away from Jesus Christ. When we are separated for the Lord we will discern the difference between our voice, the enemy's voice, and the voice of Our God; our voice brings confusion, the enemy's voice comes to steal, kill and destroy, and God's voice gives life and peace.

We need to be like Prophet Samuel moving in the realm of the spirit, able to see the past, the present, and the future. Let's look at the Prophet Samuel in I Samuel 8:19, "And Samuel answered Saul, and said, I am the seer: go up before me unto the high place; for ye shall eat with me today and tomorrow I will let thee go, and will tell thee all that is in thine heart." And then in I Samuel 9:1-9 Prophet Samuel anointed Saul and told him the past about his father losing his asses, the present; the Lord anointed him to be king over Israel, and the future; that when Saul aparted from him, he would come across three men carrying three loaves of bread, etc. Now, that's a Prophet of God moving in the realm of the spirit like God wants all of us to be. When we are separated for God we can have that boldness like Prophet Samuel when he said in I Samuel 8:19, "….and I will tell thee all that is in thine heart."

We need to discern just like John the Baptist. He was separated in the wilderness for the Lord and when the Pharisees and Sadducees came to him instantly he knew them by the spirit; they may have looked good on the outside but on the inside they were rotten. He said in Matthew 3:7, "But when he saw many of the Pharisees and Sadducees come to his baptism, he said unto them, O generation of vipers, who hath warned you to flee from the wrath to come?" In other words a Prophet should be separated walking in holiness unto the Lord so they are able to hear clearly from the Lord at anytime.

A Prophet will see things before they happen as it says in Amos 3:7, "Surely the Lord God will do nothing, but he revealeth his secret unto his servants the prophets." Prophet Ahijah was a prophet separated for the Lord and even though his eyesight was not that great the Lord showed him in the spirit before things happened. I Kings 14:1-13, shows how King Jeroboam had told his wife to disguise herself and go to the Prophet to see if God was going to heal their son. God had already spoken to the Prophet that King Jeroboam was in sin and to give him the word of the Lord. Verses 4-6, "And Jeroboam's wife did so, and arose, and went to Shiloh, and came to the house of Ahijah. But Ahijah could not see; for his eyes were set by reason of his age. And the Lord said unto Ahijah, Behold, the wife of Jeroboam cometh to ask a thing of thee for her son; for he is sick: thus and thus shalt thou say unto her:

for it shall be, when she cometh in, that she shall feign herself to be another woman. And it was so, when Ahijah heard the sound of her feet, as she came in at the door, that he said, Come in, thou wife of Jeroboam; why feignest thou thyself to be another? For I am sent to thee with heavy tidings." Prophet Isaiah was a Prophet used mighty in foretelling of the future; he prophesied of John the Baptist coming, of Jesus birth, of Jesus visiting the land of Zabulon and Nephthalim of Jesus baring our infirmities and sicknesses, and he prophesied of the religious people who don't accept the move of the Holy Spirit, and many more. (Matthew 4:14, Matthew 8:16, 17, Luke 3:4, Luke 4:17, John 1:23, 24, John 12:38-41)

Another way God reveals these secrets and speaks to the Prophets is through dreams and visions. Numbers 12:6, "And he said, Hear now my words: If there be a prophet among you, I the Lord will make myself known unto him in a vision, and will speak unto him in a dream." God gives understanding and insight through dreams and visions. In Job 33:15-17 the Word explains how God will impart and instruct us in His ways even while we sleep. God is able to speak to our spirit man, which does not sleep to guide us.

A Prophet in the middle part of the pool likes trouble for this reason because they know that when they go into a person's life, a church, a nation, or wherever they are sent that the Lord will guide and direct them with His wisdom. Therefore, they will be used by the Lord Jesus to help the Body of Christ to get out of their situation, dilemma, or circumstance. A good example of this is in Acts 15:22-32 when the Apostles Paul and Barnabas sent forth the Prophets Judas and Silas to bring a message of correction to the church in Antioch because people were trying to bring them back under the law and put the church in bondage in regards to circumcision. Verses 30-32 says, "So when they were dismissed, they came to Antioch: and when they had gathered the multitude together, they delivered the epistle: which when they had read, they rejoiced for the consolation. And Judas and Silas being prophets also themselves, exhorted the brethren with many words and confirmed them." As Prophets of God we need to like confrontation so that we can speak the Word of the Lord no matter the situation so change can come about and God be glorified.

Jeremiah 1:10 shows the work that a Prophet does, "See, I have this day set thee over the nations and over the kingdoms, to root out, and to pull down, and to destroy, and to throw down, to build, and to plant." You may be saying, "Well what needs to be rooted out, pulled down, destroyed, and then built and planted?" The answer is every religious root, every false doctrine or teaching, any anger, bitterness, unforgiveness, anything that is not established by the word of God and pointing you to Jesus Christ and a closer walk with Him needs to be rooted out, pulled down, and destroyed so that Jesus Christ can be all in all in your life. The building and the planting comes by impartation of the gifts of the spirit and the revelations of the Word of God. See, God had called Prophet Jeremiah, like He is calling many of you to be Prophets to the nations. Jeremiah 1:5 says, "Before I formed thee (put your name in there) in the belly, I knew thee, and before thou camest forth out of the womb I sanctified thee, and I ordained thee a Prophet unto the nations." Prophets are used to prepare the way of the Lord's return; that the body of Christ will be ready. (Ephesians 5:27, "That he might present it to himself a glorious church, not having spot, or wrinkle, or any such thing; but that it should be holy and without blemish.")

A Prophet in the middle part of the pool is able to discern the gifts and calling God has placed on a person's life and then they go in like a cattleman that brands their cattle to show ownership; the Prophet goes in to brand the hearts of God's people to have a loving hunger and desire for Him, a passion for the Word of God, and a longing to fulfill the call of God in their lives.

A Prophet is able to foretell and forth tell. You may be questioning what is that for—Well, Foretelling is prophecy, telling something before it happens. The Prophet Agabus in Acts 11:27, 28 foretold of the coming of a great famine in the land. "And in these days came prophets from Jerusalem unto Antioch. And there stood up one of them named Agabus, and signified by the Spirit that there should be great dearth throughout all the world: which came to pass in the days of Claudius Caesar." We can see that the Word of God even tells us when this prophecy that was foretold came to pass. Many things for the future have been foretold as you can clearly see throughout the book of Revelations; that is foretelling what will happen.—Forth telling is bringing to light what is happening and how it relates to the Word of God. An example of forth telling is in Luke 4:17-21, "And there was delivered unto him the book of the Prophet Esaias. And when he had opened the book, he found the place where it was written, the Spirit of the Lord is upon me, because he hath anointed me to preach the gospel to the poor; he hath sent me to heal the broken hearted, to preach deliverance to the captives, and recovering of sight to the blind, to set at liberty them that are bruised, to preach the acceptable year of the Lord. And he closed the book, and he gave it again to the minister, and sat down. And the eyes of all them that were in the synagogue were fastened on him. And he began to say unto them, this day is this scripture fulfilled in your ears." What Jesus was saying is that He, Himself was the fulfillment of the prophetic word spoken by the Prophet Isaiah, and He was standing there right before them. Forth Telling is bringing to light the understanding of the Word of God or a prophetic word.

Prophets were also known as seers because they moved in dreams and visions. I Samuel 9:9 says, "Beforetime in Israel, when a man went to inquire of God thus he spake, Come, and let us go to the seer: for he that is now called a Prophet was beforetime called a Seer." Prophet Elisha moved mightily in visions and he was a true watchman for God's people. Prophet Elisha was separated for the Lord and he would hear the plans of attack that the King of Syria had against God's people and he would give God's people warning. Because of this the King of Syria was angry and sent a great host of men with horses and chariots against the Prophet Elisha. (II Kings 6:8-17) The Prophet Elisha didn't even move he stayed cool, calm and collected because he could also see that the mountain was full of horses and chariots of fire from the Lord. The Prophet Elisha also stood on the Word of God knowing that "If God is for us, who can be against us." (Romans 8:31) Prophet Elisha's servant began to be fearful when he saw the enemy that had come up against them because the servant's eyesight in the realm of the spirit had not yet been open. So, Prophet Elisha prayed that the Lord would also open up the eyes of his servant as I pray for each of you also now that are just stepping into your call as a Prophet of God. "And Elisha prayed, and said, Lord, I pray thee, open his (your) eyes, that he may see. And the Lord opened the eyes of the young man; and he saw: and, behold the mountain was full of horses and chariots of fire round about Elisha." A Prophet that is full of the Word of God not only has the angels of the Lord encamped around them they also have a wall of protection, a Wall of Fire. Zechariah 2:5, "For I, saith the Lord, will be unto her a wall of fire round about and will be the glory in the midst of her." A Prophet that is not in love with the Word of God or full of the Word of God sounds like "Bppp-p" (a bunch of gas); – like the Word says in Jeremiah 5:13, "And the prophets shall become wind, and the word is not in them; thus shall it be done unto them." A Prophet goes in to declare, to decree, and to proclaim the Word of the Lord. A Prophet draws people unto repentance to Prepare the Way of the Lord.

You may be thinking that I haven't mentioned the deep end of the pool in explaining the prophetic; but here it is… the deep end of the pool is a Prophet but it is also an Apostle. An Apostle is a Prophet moving in the deep calling unto deep. Just like I mentioned before that a Prophet brings the anointing into the church; we need to understand that an Apostle takes the church from Glory to Glory. An Apostle having the heart of God is able to declare the edict and verdict of the judgment of God.

Apostles

Apostles are ones sent forth. Apostles receive the call of God by a visitation. You may be asking yourself, "How is that possible?" Let's look at the life of Apostle Paul, who was called after Jesus Christ ascended into the heavens. Turn with me in the Word of God and let us read in Acts 9:1-20. Remember that Apostle Paul's name before his conversion was Saul. We also need to realize that Saul was a Pharisee, a religious leader, who had a zeal for God and he thought what he was doing, persecuting the Christians, was the will of God. John 16:2, "They shall put you out of the synagogues: yea, the time cometh, that whosoever killeth you will think that he doeth God service." The reason why I am mentioning this is because many of us don't realize that when we talk against a man or woman of God or stop any doors from being opened, we are doing the same thing Saul did and we do not know who Jesus Christ is. When Saul had this visitation from the Lord, it was in the realm of the spirit. Notice what Jesus said to him, "Saul, Saul, why persecutest thou me?" Jesus didn't say why are you persecuting my disciples. Right away, Saul knowing the Old Testament realized that this was the Lord because he knew God spoke thru thunder and lightening. Read Exodus 20:18, 19, "And all the people saw the thunderings, and the lightenings, and the noise of the trumpet, and the mountain smoking and when the people saw it, they removed, and stood afar off. And they said unto Moses, Speak thou with us, and we will hear: but let not God speak with us, lest we die." When Saul had this encounter with the Lord Jesus, this is where his Apostolic calling began; when he received the revelation that the Lord Jesus Christ is God.

The Word of God shows us in Numbers 12:6-8, "And he said, Hear now my words: If there be a prophet among you, I the Lord will make myself known unto him in a vision, and will speak unto him in a dream. My servant Moses is not so, who is faithful in all mine house. With him will I speak mouth to mouth, even apparently, and not in dark speeches; and the similitude of the Lord shall he behold: wherefore then were ye not afraid to speak against my servant Moses?" Moses was representative of the Apostolic, Father figure just like Abraham. Notice how God said he will speak mouth to mouth; that means an encounter or a visitation. (Fathers represent the Apostolic) Let's look at the times God came to Abraham, the Father of Many Nations. Genesis 12:7 says, "And the Lord appeared unto Abram, and said, unto thy seed will I give this land: and there builded he an altar unto the Lord, who appeared unto him." Genesis 17:1 says, "And when Abram was ninety years old and nine, the Lord appeared to Abram, and said unto him, I am the Almighty God; walk before me, and be thou perfect." Genesis 18:1 says, "And the Lord appeared unto him in the plains of Mamre; and he sat in the tent door in the heat of the day." In other words, an Apostle will have an encounter with the Lord three times. The first time God came to Abram, God was setting forth the call of God in Abram's life; the second time, God ordained and activated the gifts and callings in Abram's life; and the third time, God sent forth Abraham by His Spirit to fulfill the call of God in his life. Apostle Paul also had three encounters: First, in Acts Chapter 9 on the road to Damascus. Second, when he separated himself for the Lord as it says in Galatians 1:15, 16, "But when it pleased God, who separated me from my mother's womb, and called me by his grace, to reveal his Son in me, that I might preach him among the heathen; immediately I conferred not with flesh and blood." Thirdly, when God took Apostle Paul into the third heaven to show him mighty revelations. II Corinthians 12:2, "I knew a man in Christ above fourteen years ago, (whether in the body, I cannot tell; or whether out of the body, I cannot tell: God knoweth;) such an one caught up to the third heaven." Then God sent him forth by His Spirit as it says in Acts 13:1, 2. In the Old Testament, Abraham, Moses, Noah, etc. were only representative of the Apostolic because Jesus Christ is the First Apostle as mentioned in Hebrews 3:1 to bring order into the church. Remember, we, the body of Christ, are the church.

Apostles have a universal view and vision for the Body of Christ. Apostles are like architects they see the whole picture. (From the blue print all the way to the completion of the house.) Apostle Paul referred to himself that way when he called himself a master builder. I Corinthians 3:10, "According to the grace of God which is given unto me, as a wise masterbuilder, I have laid the foundation, and another buildeth thereon. But let every man take heed how he buildeth thereupon." The Apostles not only see the forest, they observe each tree in the forest and the characteristics of each tree. In other words the Apostles will be able to determine by the Spirit of the Living God the gifts and callings of each individual and to activate them. Such as Apostle Paul has written in II Timothy 1:6, where the Apostle Paul speaks of himself laying his hands upon Timothy for ordination; "Wherefore I put thee in remembrance that thou stir up the gift of God, which is in thee by the putting on of my hands." You can see, that Timothy was called and ordained to be an Evangelist; II Timothy 4:5, "But watch thou in all things, endure afflictions, do the work of an evangelist, make full proof of thy ministry." Apostles are used to impart and activate spiritual gifts as Apostle Paul wrote in Romans 1:11, "For I long to see you, that I may impart unto you some spiritual gift, to the end ye may be established."

Apostles are our spiritual Fathers; Malachi 4:6, "And he shall turn the heart of the fathers to the children, and the heart of the children to their fathers, lest I come and smite the earth with a curse." We need our spiritual Fathers for correction and chastisement. For without chastisement where is the love. Hebrews 12:6-8, "For whom the Lord loveth he chasteneth, and scourgeth every son whom he receiveth. If ye endure chastening, God dealeth with you as with sons; for what son is he whom the father chasteneth not? But if ye be without chastisement, whereof all are partakers, then are ye bastards and not sons." Notice what the Apostle Paul says in I Corinthians 4:15, "For thou you have ten thousand instructors in Christ, yet have ye not many fathers: for in Christ Jesus I have begotten you through the gospel." We need our Spiritual Fathers to pull our ears when we are going the wrong way. Apostles are encouragers like Barnabas; as much as we need the chastisement, we also need the encouragement. That is why they are like builders because through encouragement we receive strength to continue on. Apostles are overseers, used to govern the body of Christ.

Apostles, as well as prophets, are able to receive the revelations from the Word of God. Ephesians 3:1-5, "For this cause I Paul, the prisoner of Jesus Christ for you Gentiles, If you have heard of the dispensation of the grace of God which is given me to you-ward: how that by revelation He made known unto me the mystery; (as I wrote afore in few words, whereby, when ye read, ye may understand my knowledge in the mystery of Christ.) Which in other ages was not made known unto the sons of men, as it is now revealed unto his holy apostles and prophets by the Spirit." An example of this is in the book of Acts on the day of Pentecost when the people saw 120 men and women baptized in the Holy Ghost and because of lack of understanding they thought they were drunk. Apostle Peter having grabbed the revelation, stood up and brought forth the revelation of what the Prophet Joel had prophesied in Joel 2:28-32. Look what it says in Acts 2:1-16, "And when the day of Pentecost was fully come, they were all with one accord in one place. And suddenly there came a sound from heaven as of a rushing mighty wind, and it filled all the house where they were sitting. And there appeared unto them cloven tongues like as of fire, and it sat upon each of them. And they were all filled with the Holy Ghost, and began to speak with other tongues, as the Spirit gave them utterance. And there were dwelling at Jerusalem Jews, devout men, out of every nation under heaven. Now when this was noised abroad, the multitude came together and were confounded, because that every man heard them speak in his own language. And they were all amazed and marveled, saying one to another, Behold, are not all these which speak Galilaeans? And how hear we every man in our own tongue, wherein we were born? Parthians, and Medes, and Elamites, and the dwellers in Mesopotamia and in Judaea, and Cappadocia, in Pontus and Asia, Phrygia, and Pamphylia in Egypt, and in the parts of Libya about Cyrene, and strangers of Rome, Jews and proselytes, Cretes and Arabians, we do hear them speak in our tongues the wonderful works of God. And they were all amazed, and were in doubt, saying one to another, "What meaneth this? Others mocking said, "These men are full of new wine. But Peter, standing up with the eleven, lifted up his voice, and said unto them, Ye men of Judaea, and all ye that dwell at Jerusalem, be this known unto you, and hearken to my words: For these are not drunken, as ye suppose, seeing it is but the third hour of the day. But this is that which was spoken by the Prophet Joel." The Apostle Peter brought forth the understanding of the Baptism of the Holy Spirit by bringing forth the revelation of the prophecy. It is only by the revelations of the Word of God that we are able to go from glory to glory.

The Apostles, as well as prophets, are the foundations for the Body of Christ (which is the Church). Ephesians 2:20, "And are built upon the foundation of the apostles and prophets, Jesus Christ Himself being the chief corner stone." A building without a foundation cannot stand and that is the same for us being the church built without hands as the Word of God says in II Corinthians 5:1. The Apostles go in first and come out last when it comes to establishing the foundations and then building a platform for the Prophets. Building a platform means that when the Prophets get a prophetic word and present it to the Apostles; the Apostles chew on it to see exactly what the Lord is speaking, listen to the Lord and then release the prophetic word or release the Prophet to speak in God's timing.

Apostles have a universal vision and that is important for the establishing of the church. We need the blessings of Our Spiritual Fathers; in other words, we need to have the covering of an Apostle and to be sent out by them. Romans 10:15 states, "And how shall they preach except they be sent?" See God the Father sent His Son and His Son, Jesus, sent the Holy Spirit and by the Spirit of the Living God the Apostles are sent forth. Read Acts 13:1, 2 when the prophets, the teachers and the men and women of God were in prayer and fasting the Holy Ghost sent forth Barnabas and Saul. "Now there were in the church that was at Antioch certain prophets and teachers; as Barnabas, and Simeon that was called Niger, and Lucius of Cyrene, and Manaen, which had been brought up with Herod the tetrarch, and Saul. As they ministered to the Lord, and fasted, the Holy Ghost said, "Separate me Barnabas and Saul for the work whereunto I have called them." This is a beautiful illustration of how we need to be sent out. The Apostles then impart, activate, ordain and send forth the Prophets, the

Evangelists, the Pastors, and the Teachers to do the work of the Lord. There is another illustration in the Old Testament in Genesis Chapter 24, where Abraham sent forth his servant, to go get a wife for his son, Isaac. Abraham represents the Father, the servant represents the Holy Spirit and Isaac represents the son, Our Lord and Savior Jesus Christ, and the wife (the bride) represents the church. When Abraham sent forth his servant, this is representative of what God the Father did for us; God the Father sent forth the Holy Spirit to get a Bride for His son, Jesus Christ. When you read Genesis chapter 24, you will notice that the father, Abraham, made the covenant with his servant to bring back the bride. He also told the servant if she is not willing to come that you are free from this oath in Genesis 24:8. This is showing us here we have a choice. When we are sent out by our apostolic covering, we are under the protection of the Lord and we will have the wall of fire about us, as it says in Zechariah 2:5, "For I, saith the Lord, will be unto her a wall of fire round about, and will be the glory in the midst of her." The characteristics of an Apostle and Prophet are found in I Samuel 16:18 "...that is cunning in playing, and a mighty valiant man, and a man of war, and prudent in matters, and a comely person, and the Lord is with him." We need to know how to praise, worship, and glorify the Lord. We need to be strong in character knowing who Our God is and who we are in Him and be willing to lose it all to gain it all. We need to be warriors and generals for Jesus; not afraid of confrontation or afraid to confront a situation, no matter who it is. We need to know how to speak prudently and in the timing of the Lord; declaring what the Lord has to say. We need to be attractive....that means because we are washed by the Blood of Jesus Christ and because we carry the Glory of the Lord in our lives that we look so good. And most importantly, we need to know the Lord is with us.

Apostles are trailblazers and pioneers going in to establish the five-fold ministry in places. Some people think this means building a lot of buildings. No, what God wants is the five-fold ministry established so God's people can be perfected. Apostles are able to close the gates of hell as written in Matthew 16:18, "...and the gates of hell shall not prevail against it." An example of this is when my husband, who is an Apostle of God, heard his mother had been hurt and was not expected to live long. While praying, we heard she needed to repent and reconcile her life to the Lord. Immediately, my husband, an Apostle, closed the gates of hell until his sister was able to go minister to their mother. Also, the Apostles are able to open the heavens. This power and authority was given when Jesus said in John 20:23, "Whose soever sins ye remit they are remitted unto them; and whose soever sins ye retain, they are retained."

So as you can see, Apostles are foundations used to establish, govern, activate, ordain, impart, build, encourage, strengthen, to teach, to send forth and to bring order in the Body of Christ. Both the Apostles and the Prophets are the foundations we need to build on, as the Word of God says in Ephesians 2:20. When we have the foundations established, we can rejoice and celebrate like the people of Israel did in the book of Ezra 3:10, 11, "And when the builders laid the foundation of the temple of the Lord, they set the priests in their apparel with trumpets, and the Levites, the sons of Asaph with cymbals, to praise the Lord, after the ordinance of David king of Israel. And they sang together by course in praising and giving thanks unto the Lord; because he is good, for his mercy endureth for ever toward Israel. And all the people shouted with a great shout, when they praised the foundation of the house of the Lord was laid." In understanding Our God, when we praise the Lord, He is sitting on His throne inhaling the praises. As Our God inhales the praises, He is also exhaling revelations upon revelations for us to grow in Him. Glory to God, forever! Only by the Apostolic, which is a Prophet moving in the deep end of the pool, can judgment be brought forth. An example is in I Corinthians 5:1-5 when the Apostle Paul had heard of the sexual perversion going on amongst the believers in Corinth. He declared in verse 5, "To deliver such an one unto Satan for the destruction of the flesh, that the spirit may be saved in the day of the Lord Jesus." Apostle Paul was not only concerned for the soul of that individual but also for that whole body of believers. He goes on to say in verses 6 and 7 to purge out the leaven (the sin) because a little leaven, leaveneth the whole lump. To some of you this may sound harsh; when Apostle Paul turned that man over to satan, but if you understand the realm of the spirit, this was so that man and all that were around him would get their lives right with the Lord and not go to hell.

When we have the five-fold ministry operating together for the Glory of the Lord, the enemy will not be able to stop us in building God's kingdom. Remember what Jesus said in Matthew 16:18, "And I say also unto thee, that thou art Peter, and upon this rock I will build my church; and the gates of hell shall not prevail against it." Let it be so, that we allow the five-fold ministry working together to destroy the works of the enemy that the Gates of Hell Shall Not Prevail. Praise the name of Our Lord and Savior, Jesus Christ, forever!

UNDERSTANDING THE
SPIRITUAL REALM AND THE
SEER ANOINTING

God spoke and prophesied through the Prophet Joel that the Spirit of the Lord would be moving mighty in the last days. The Word of God shows us that God is outpouring His Spirit on all mankind. Joel 2:28-32, "And it shall come to pass afterward, that I will pour out my spirit upon all flesh: and your sons and your daughters shall prophesy, your old men shall dream dreams, your young men shall see visions: And also upon the servants and upon the handmaids in those days will I pour out my spirit. And I will shew wonders in the heavens and in the earth, blood, and fire, and pillars of smoke. The sun shall be turned into darkness, and the moon into blood, before the great and the terrible day of the Lord come. And it shall come to pass, that whosoever shall call on the name of the Lord shall be delivered: for in mount Zion and in Jerusalem shall be deliverance, as the Lord hath said, and in the remnant whom the Lord shall call." The prophetic word that the Prophet Joel spoke is being fulfilled. However, it is up to us to get what God the Father, God the Son, and God the Holy Spirit have for us. Prophecy takes action on our part. God speaks but we have to go get it. An example of this is in I Samuel 30:8; God told David he would recover all. It took David believing and going for it in order for the prophecy to be fulfilled. The Word of God shows us in Ephesians 1:11 that we have an inheritance of which the only way we can obtain that is by us being in the spirit. I Samuel 30:9-19 shows it was fulfilled. The problem with many of us is that we are sitting around waiting for God to just dump it in our laps instead of doing what we need to do so that God will complete the prophetic word in our lives. God had spoken prophetically in I Samuel 16:12, 13 to David that he would be king over all Israel; this was fulfilled in I Chronicles 11:3 after David had gone through many, many, many trials. In other words, David had to act on that prophetic word in order for prophecy to be fulfilled.

Remember, in order for the Israelites to enter into the Promise Land they had to be circumcised; this is when Joshua said drop your pants so the flesh can be cut off. (Joshua 5:2) It is the same for us today. We have to have our hearts circumcised that we walk not after the flesh but after the spirit. We need to go get all that the Lord Jesus Christ has for us thru the Spirit and use it. Notice that in the prophetic word spoken by Joel the scripture says, "Whosoever shall call on the name of the Lord shall be delivered." God chose to use us who believe for that work as it says in Mark 16:16-18, "He that believeth and is baptized shall be saved; but he that believeth not shall be damned. And these signs shall follow them that believe; in my name shall they cast out devils; they shall speak with new tongues; they shall take up serpents; and if they drink any deadly thing, it shall not hurt them; they shall lay hands on the sick, and they shall recover." You need to ask yourself, "Do you believe?" And if yes, are these signs and wonders following you? Jesus said when He was on the cross, "It is finished." He finished what God the Father sent Him here for and when He ascended into heaven, He sent us the Holy Spirit, The Helper, so that we can receive all He has for us. It is now up to us to go get it!! So, if these signs and wonders are not yet following your life, get up and go get the promises of God for your life.

Saul, who later became the Apostle Paul, in Acts 9:1-18 had the encounter with Jesus Christ and the Lord still chose to use a man of God, Ananias, to lay hands on Saul so that the scales fell from his eyes and he received his deliverance. Jesus chose to use his disciples to deliver Lazarus, Mary and Martha's brother; when Lazarus had risen from the dead. Jesus called Lazarus forth from the grave saying, "Lazarus come forth," as Lazarus came forth he was still wearing his grave clothes and Jesus told the disciples, "Loose him, and let him go." (John 11:43, 44) Jesus used His disciples to deliver Lazarus. By us moving powerfully in the prophetic seer anointing God can use each one of us for the deliverance of His people. However, in order for God to use us we need to have that relationship with God the Father, God the Son and

God the Holy Spirit. We need to know who our enemy is as well as his tactics. Another secret to moving powerfully in the seer anointing, first of all, is having the Word of God in you richly; because Hebrews 4:12 says, the Word of God is "a discerner of the thoughts and intents of the heart. Secondly, apply the blood of Jesus over that person or person's heart (that everything hidden shall be revealed.) Thirdly, declaring I Corinthians 14:25 over their lives. I Corinthians 14:25 says, "And thus are the secrets of his heart made manifest; and so falling down on his face, he will worship God, and report that God is in you of a truth." We need to be like the Prophet Elisha moving in such a realm of the spirit that our spirit can go into someone else's spirit to truly know them and what they are struggling with. Let's look in II Kings 5:15-26. When Prophet Elisha had spoken the prophetic word to Naaman, captain of the host of Syria; Naaman fulfilled the prophetic word and God healed him of leprosy. Then Naaman returned to the Prophet Elisha to give him a reward. Prophet Elisha refused to accept the gift because Naaman did not give it initially as a gift of faith but waited till he received his healing. Prophet Elisha refused the gift because God and the things of God cannot be bought. However, Gehazi, the servant of Prophet Elisha, had a door open in his heart for covetness and went back to Naaman and lied to him to receive the gift. Prophet Elisha had gone with him in the spirit; verses 25, 26, "But he went in and stood before his master. And Elisha said unto him, whence comest thou, Gehazi? And he said, "Thy servant went no whither." And he said unto him, "Went not mine heart with thee, when the man turned again from his chariot to meet thee? Is it time to receive money, and to receive garments, and oliveyards, and vineyards, and sheep, and oxen, and menservants, and maidservants?" By Prophet Elisha moving in that realm of the spirit he was able to see that Gehazi was struggling with a spirit of greed and covetness. We can know someone by their spirit....I Corinthians 2:11, "For what man knoweth the things of a man, save the spirit of man which is in him? Even so the things of God knoweth no man but the Spirit of God."

Just like Jesus, as the Word says, was touched by the feelings of our infirmities. Hebrews 4:15, "For we have not an high priest which cannot be touched with the feeling of our infirmities; but was in all points tempted like as we are, yet without sin." I believe that is why He allows us to feel what is going on with others through the Word of Knowledge and also, I believe because we are all of one body - The Body of Christ. If you know how to listen and hear in the realm of the spirit, you can hear when someone's spirit is crying to the Lord. An example of this is while praying for one of the Prophets in our ministry, I heard what her spirit was saying to God and I felt the Lord give me the answer for her. She began to weep for joy because of the awesomeness of Our God.

These are awesome days for the Preparing of the Way of the Lord.... thru God's Spirit; He has given us giftings and we need to understand them and understand how to use them. In this chapter we shall be speaking about the Prophetic Anointing. In the Prophetic Anointing there is what is called the Knoby and the Seer Anointing (I Samuel 9:9). The Knoby is when something is put in your spirit and you just know that you know that you know that it is from the Lord. Knoby is just a prophetic term for knowing or knowledge; a revelation from God. In the Old Testament it is referred to as the Urim and Thummin, which was worn upon the priests' breastplate. Exodus 28:30, "And thou shalt put in the breastplate of judgment the Urim and the Thummim; and they shall be upon Aaron's heart, when he goeth in before the Lord: and Aaron shall bear the judgment of the children of Israel upon his heart before the Lord continually." The judgment God is referring to is not for condemnation but to help God's people get out of their situations or dilemmas and the only way we can do that is by spiritually discerning what is happening in that person's life. We need to speak what the Lord has to say; not watering the Word of God down or sugar coating it but with the grace and mercy of the Lord that their souls be saved. People are going to think you are hard at times; remember in Jeremiah 23:29, "Is not my word like as a fire? Saith the Lord; and like a hammer that breaketh the rock in pieces?" The Word of God is like a fire to burn out all the chaff, anything that is not of the Lord. The Word of God is also like a hammer when someone is in sin. No matter the cost, we need to speak what the Lord says. We are not here to make friends but to do the Will of the Father; the Word says in James 4:4, "...whosoever therefore will be a friend of the world is the enemy of God." If we are here to make friends take note as to what Luke 6:26 says, "Woe unto you, when all men shall speak well of you! For so did their fathers to the false prophets." True Christ love is telling the person the truth so that they won't go to hell. Proverbs 27:5, 6 says,

"Open rebuke is better than secret love. Faithful are the wounds of a friend; but the kisses of an enemy are deceitful." When we do it God's way there is great reward. James 5:20 says, "Let him know, that he which converteth the sinner from the error of his way, shall save a soul from death, and shall hide a multitude of sins." Having said all this, let us remember to not look at or judge people with our own eyes or by the flesh. Isaiah 11:3, "And shall make him of quick understanding in the fear of the Lord: and he shall not judge after the sight of his eyes, neither reprove after the hearing of his ears." The religious spirit will always say "you're judging me, you're judging me etc;" however, when someone wants to get right with the Lord they have ears to hear what the Spirit is saying. The Word of God says in I Corinthians 5:11-13 that if we call ourselves a brother or sister in Christ we are to judge each other rightly; to be a watchman for the Lord

The Seer Anointing has many avenues. Sometimes God will show you things thru visions, dreams, or even thru the Word of Knowledge, which is one of the nine gifts of the Spirit mentioned in I Corinthians 12:7-11. Sometimes through the Prophetic Tongue and the Interpretation of Tongues God will reveal what is going on. These two are also of the nine gifts of the Spirit. This also happened in the Old Testament in the book of Daniel chapter 5 when the handwriting came on the wall and the Spirit of the Living God gave Prophet Daniel the Interpretation revealing what God had to say in the situation. We will go into each area and share with you how God showed us. Remember God is an Awesome God and He speaks in various ways so He may show you these things in different ways. Use this only for guidance, as a tool for understanding. God will also show us things through the use of our five senses. The Word of God says in Hebrews 5:13, 14, "For every one that useth milk is unskillful in the word of righteousness: for he is a babe. But strong meat belongeth to them that are of full age, even those who by reason of use have their senses exercised to discern both good and evil." This refers to Hearing, Seeing, Smelling, Tasting, and Touching. As Prophets of God, when you are discerning in the realm of the spirit, first of all, regarding smelling, the things of God have a sweet aroma but the things of the enemy have a foul odor. Isaiah 3:24, "And it shall come to pass, that instead of sweet smell there shall be stink; and instead of a girdle a rent; and instead of well set hair baldness; and instead of a stomacher a girding of sackcloth; and burning instead of beauty." The same goes for any of our senses that we are using to discern; the good is of the Lord and that which is foul, tastes bad, looks evil etc. is from the enemy. When it comes to listening, as Jesus said, be careful how you hear. We need to receive that which is good, and let the words of the enemy fall to the ground. In the book of Judges 7:13-15; God allowed Gideon to overhear a Midianite speaking about a dream he had and the interpretation that God was going to deliver the Midianites into the hands of Gideon. This was all ordered by God to bring encouragement to Gideon, the man of God. Remember always to compare what you see, hear, smell, taste, or touch with the Word of God; for the Bible says that we will worship Him in Spirit and Truth in John 4:23. All of God's giftings and the calling of God in your lives are to bring Glory and Honor and Praise unto Jesus Christ.

The spiritual realm is awesome! We must remember, however, that Satan is an imitator. He will use anyone that has an open door in their hearts. II Corinthians 11:14 says, "And no marvel; for Satan himself is transformed into an angel of light." In Matthew 16:21-23, Jesus began to tell his disciples how He must go to Jerusalem and suffer many things and be killed for us. Peter, not understanding and having an open door for pride (I believe) because a few verses before, had spoken the awesome revelation that he had received from the Father that Jesus is the Christ. So, satan used him to go against the plans of God and Jesus began to rebuke him. Jesus then answers Peter in verse 23, "But he turned, and said unto Peter, Get thee behind me, Satan; thou art an offense unto me: for thou savourest not the things that be of God, but those that be of men." Many times when God uses us mightily, the enemy comes right after to try to get us to receive the glory. That is a spirit of pride.

Another incident was when a young man came to us for deliverance and there was another man of God that was with us when this young man came in. The other man of God that was with us was not moving in discernment, so when he saw this young man walk in he made a statement, "Wow, this young guy looks really good." The young man that came in for deliverance had such a heavy, heavy spirit of lust that the man of God thought it was a glow of the Lord. Therefore, we need to be delivered and walking in holiness so that God can speak to us clearly. We need to cry out for discernment and understanding.

Proverbs 2:3, "Yea, if thou criest after knowledge, and liftest up thy voice for understanding;" surely the Lord will answer.

We need to develop our relationship with the Holy Spirit. When you get a Word of Knowledge learn to ask the Spirit of Truth questions. First of all ask, "Is this for me or someone else?" Listen, discern, and test the spirit. The way to test the spirit is as it says in I John 4:1-3, "Beloved, believe not every spirit, but try the spirits whether they are of God: because many false prophets are gone out into the world. Hereby know ye the Spirit of God: Every spirit that confesseth that Jesus Christ is come in the flesh is of God: And every spirit that confesseth not that Jesus Christ is come in the flesh is not of God and this is that spirit of antichrist, whereof ye have heard that it should come; and even now already is it in the world." So after you hear something, just say within yourself, "Did Jesus come in the flesh? If you hear yes, you know that this is from the Lord and not from an evil spirit. We need to practice so that we develop our listening to the Spirit of Truth. Jesus told the disciples in John 16:7, "Nevertheless I tell you the truth; it is expedient for you that I go away: for if I go not away, the Comforter will not come unto you; but if I depart, I will send him unto you." How blessed we are that the Holy Spirit dwells within us that we can have that relationship with Him all the time. There are three voices: Our voice, the enemy's voice, and the Spirit of the Lord (the voice of God). Our voice will bring confusion, the enemy's voice will bring deception, whereas God's voice will bring peace and will agree with the Word of God. The book of James 3:17 tells us how the wisdom from God is: "But the wisdom that is from above is first pure, then peaceable, gentle, and easy to be entreated, full of mercy and good fruits, without partiality, and without hypocrisy."

God will allow us to be tested when He gives us a prophetic word. If you are under an Apostolic covering, living separated for the Lord, and spending time with the Lord, learn to stand on the Word of the Lord that God has given you for your life. You may be saying, "Why am I telling you this?" Let's turn to I Kings 13:1-24; The Prophet of Judah was used powerfully by God to give a word to King Jeroboam and was told by God to leave after giving the Word. This Prophet of Judah was moving in signs and wonders when he declared that the altar, King Jeroboam had been using to make sacrifices to other gods, would be rent by God Almighty. He declared that altar would be turned into ashes and it happened right before King Jeroboam's eyes. The Prophet of Judah also declared the name of the king (Josiah) that God was going to raise up for himself to bring order to His people. Even when King Jeroboam tried to go against the Prophet of Judah the judgment of God came immediately and his hand dried up that he could not pull it in again to him until the Prophet of Judah prayed for him. But look what happened when God allowed the Word of the Lord spoken to him to be tested. Let us read I Kings 13:7-9, "And the king said unto the man of God, Come home with me, and refresh thyself, and I will give thee a reward. And the man of God said unto the king, If thou wilt give me half thine house, I will not go in with thee, neither will I eat bread nor drink water in this place: for so was it charged me by the word of the Lord, saying, eat no bread, nor drink water, nor turn again by the same way that thou camest." The Prophet of Judah had declared what the Lord had said to him. However, when another prophet had come to him; God allowed the test to come to see if the Prophet of Judah would stand upon the Word of the Lord. Read verse 18; "He said unto him, I am a prophet also as thou art; and an angel spake unto me by the word of the Lord, saying, bring him back with thee into thine house, that he may eat bread and drink water. But he lied unto him." This caused the Prophet of Judah's life to be shortened. Read the whole chapter. That is why the Apostle Paul said in Galatians 1:8, "But though we, or an angel from heaven, preach any other gospel unto you than that which we have preached unto you, let him be accursed." We need to learn to listen to the spirit and stand on the Word God has spoken for our lives. The only way you're going to be able to do that is if you are separated for the Lord Jesus and spending your time in the Word of God. Remember also, when John the Baptist baptized Jesus, the heavens were open, the Holy Spirit descended like a dove, and lighting upon him: and lo a voice from heaven saying, "This is my beloved Son, in whom I am well pleased." (Matthew 3:16, 17) Immediately after this, the Spirit led Jesus into the wilderness and He, Jesus, being God, was allowed to be tested by the devil. The very words that God the Father spoke to Him the enemy tried to put question to. The devil said in Matthew 4:3 "And when the tempter came to him, he said, "If thou be the Son of God, command that these stones be made bread." Notice the tempter said, "If thou be the Son of God;" going directly against the words God the Father had just declared. I am emphasizing this so we all learn to stand on what God has said to us. God allows the devil to have the first shot after we receive a prophetic word.

Let us go to I Corinthians 12 where the word of God speaks about the spiritual giftings God has given us. If you will notice God the Father, God the Son, and God the Holy Spirit, all being one, work in total unity all the time. The Father calls us, the Spirit draws us, and Jesus Christ gives us life. In verses 4, 5, & 6 the word says, "Now there are diversities of gifts, but the same Spirit. And there are differences of administrations, but the same Lord. And there are diversities of operations, but it is the same God which worketh all in all." These verses show how the Lord gives us the gifts thru the Holy Spirit and by us being a willing vessel, the Father uses the giftings given to us and worketh it all together for the glory of the Lord Jesus Christ to prepare His bride.

The Gift we will be speaking about now is the Word of Knowledge and some of the possible causes for people having certain infirmities. Sometimes people may feel or sense the Word of Knowledge through a pressure or a pain in their body. The pressure or pain could be revealing to you the spirit that is affecting that person or wherein lies the spirit of infirmity that they have. Let me give you an example: You could be feeling pressure in your heart, your back, or your neck or even feeling like you are going blind and these could be a Word of Knowledge for someone else. If you are ministering one on one and you begin to feel your head ache, from what the Lord has revealed to us, this is rebellion toward authority. When you are in a large congregation or crowd and receive a Word of Knowledge such as heart pain, it is because God wants you to declare His healing for that person. If you are unable to speak at that time, all you have to do is release it unto God and ask God to heal that person. Before you know it, you will have no heart pain, no back pain, or any pain because you have released it to the Lord and interceded for the person. These are ways the Lord has shown us in the realm of the spirit to understand the gifting of the Word of Knowledge. There could be various other ways the Lord may show you. Let us begin, starting from the top of the body and working down: You could feel this as pressure, pain, burning feeling, achy, jabbing, stabbing, or even numbness in the body.

The Head

Strong pressure on the top – Rebellion toward authority. (I Samuel 15:23, "For rebellion is as the sin of witchcraft, and stubbornness is as iniquity and idolatry.") Jab directly in middle top portion of head (usually right side) – direct rebellion toward spouse or spiritual authority. Also, a spirit of oppression and control because with rebellion comes witchcraft, which is a controlling spirit. The Strongman for Rebellion is a spirit of perversion. When we go against authority we are going against Jesus Christ, who is the Head of the church. I Corinthians 11:3, "But I would have you know that the head of every man is Christ; and the head of the woman is the man."

Jab top front right side – legalistic spirit.

Feels like a stick or a pole going from the base of the neck into the head – Driving Spirit, Controlling.

Pressure in back of head, right side – Evil desires.

Colossians 3:5; (Fantasy). Inordinate affection is the same as having an idol in your heart, whether it be your husband, your wife, your kids, your marriage....anything in your heart besides Jesus Christ. Example in Bible: II Samuel 13; Amnon, David's son, inordinate affection for his sister, Tamar.

Pain/Pressure at the base of head in the back – feels like it is deep inside our subconscious – represents wrong teachings, doctrines of men. Jeremiah 9:14, "But have walked after the imaginations of their own heart, and after Baalim, which their fathers taught them."

Middle of Forehead

(Pressure between the eyes)–Covenant made thru masons, shriners, eastern star – Brings in a spirit of Death.

This is where the spirit of death hit Goliath, the giant that David fought in I Samuel 17:49.

Right Temple

Distraction. Distraction from the things of God or even other areas in their lives. This word of knowledge can also be felt or seen as the fluttering eye.

*Pressure on both temples is a strong intellect and or analytical spirit.

Left Temple

Spirit of Diversion. This is different from distraction in that it is something directly diverting that person from the call or causes of God.

Band around the Forehead

Religious spirit and or Antichrist spirit. Attempts to take Christ's place. (Like wearing the thorns) Feels like a band around the head. (Matthew 28:29)

Ears

Pain in the Left Ear. Person has been avoiding what God has been trying to tell them. Zechariah 7:13 – "Therefore it is come to pass, that as he cried, and they would not hear; so they cried, and I would not hear, saith the Lord of hosts."

Pain in Right Ear – not able to hear the voice of God or you are not listening to God; instead you are listening to the enemy.

Pain in Both Ears – Tormenting Spirits, unforgiv-ness; forgiving from the head and not the heart. Matthew 18:34; the man did not want to forgive someone who owed him, even though he had been forgiven by the king. The Word says, "And his lord was wroth, and delivered him to the tormentors, till he should pay all that was due unto him."

Tingling in ears- II Kings 21:12; God's judgment is coming because of the iniquity. I Samuel 3:11 –Rebellion toward God.

Infection in Ear – negative words spoken over you, words of discouragement or bad seeds planted in you.

Eyes

Cloudy vision, or blurred – Vision for the Body of Christ or for their church has been clouded or blurred possibly by wrong teachings, trying to do it through works, or using gimmicks to attract people to their church, etc. Proverbs 29:18, "Where there is no vision, the people perish:"

Eyes very dark like steel – hardened heart like Nebuchadnezzar in Daniel 5:20, "But when his heart was lifted up, and his mind hardened in pride, he was deposed from his kingly throne, and they took his glory from him:" ★Same as wanting to be in control – Jezebel spirit.

Eye pupil very black and red veins going from it –Spirit of Condemnation. God does not give us a spirit of condemnation. Romans 8:1, "There is therefore now no condemnation to them which are in Christ Jesus, who walk not after the flesh, but after the Spirit."

Pain in the Right Eye – Zechariah 11:17, "Woe to the idol shepherd that leaveth the flock! The sword shall be upon his arm, and upon his right eye: his arm shall be clean dried up, and his right eye shall be utterly darkened." Not watching over the flock or leaving their flock unattended.

Pain or Blindness in Right Eye – Having the wrong covering. I Samuel 11:1, 2, "Then Nahash the Ammonite came up, and encamped against Jabesh-Gilead; and all the men of

Jabesh said unto Nahash, make a covenant with us, and we will serve thee. And Nahash the Ammonite answered them, on this condition will I make a covenant with you, that I may thrust out all your right eyes, and lay it for a reproach upon all Israel."

Poke in the Eye (Jabbing feeling) Someone diverting you from the truth, choosing to go the wrong way. Joshua 24:13, "Know for a certainty that the Lord God will no more drive out any of these nations from before you; but they shall be snares and traps unto you, and scourges in your sides, and thorns in your eyes . . . ."

Dull pain in back of right eye – Someone looking at life wrong by believing because of what happened to them they begin to put the blame on others; when God is trying to change them.

Eyelids Fluttering – Distraction. Hard for person to focus on things and especially the Word of God.

Eyes shifting back and forth — spirit of insanity. Feeling like you have a patch over left eye – how that person negatively views themselves.

When you see someone's eyes that are almost shut it is because they need deliverance. They need the eyes of their understanding enlightened. Ephesians 1:18.

Someone's eyes that are solid black – it is witchcraft.

Very clouded eyes means that person needs deliverance – I saw a little girl's eyes so cloudy and as I began to speak about Jesus the little girl began throwing up.

Seeing in the spirit more than one set of eyes on a person - double minded. James 1:7, 8, "For let not that man think that he shall receive any thing of the Lord. A double-minded man is unstable in all his ways." When you see in the spirit someone having multiple sets of eyes, this comes from a spirit of confusion.

Nose

Nose itching—their spirit of discernment is being affected.

Nostrils flaring – that person is trying to repress the spirit of anger; like a horse's nostrils when it gets angry.

Sinus

Pressure on sinus, spirit of anger – usually repressed anger at someone in the past. Not ever truly releasing it. There is a difference forgiving from the head and forgiving from the heart. When forgiveness is from the heart you won't cry or hurt from that situation anymore. An example of forgiving from the head and not the heart is in the book of II Samuel 24. King David had taken a census of the people, (In other words, he was allowing pride to come in measuring who he was by how many people he had following him) which was against God. Conviction came into David in verses 10-14 when Gad, David's Seer, told him what God had to say about the census. However, it wasn't until verse 17 when David's heart became broken and contrite, when he saw the judgment of God upon the people. We also have sinus cavities at the base of our skull; we ministered to a woman who had a big knot there, the Lord revealed to me that it was repressed anger toward her mother. The woman confirmed this was true, after ministering to her the Lord delivered and healed her.

Cheeks

Spirit of anger – the cheeks will be swollen. I saw the spirit of anger. Both cheeks were round and swollen with a red hue to them.

Abscess Tooth

Pain in one or more of your teeth - Bitterness has settled in. Proverbs 14:30, "....but envy the rottenness of the bones."

Tongue

> Numbness of tongue. Speaking negative words either over your own life or someone else's. Proverbs 18:21 – Death and life are in the power of the tongue.

> Taste of Silver – (Light metal tasting) Could be the Word of God is rich within them. Psalm 12:6, "The words of the Lord are pure words: as silver tried in a furnace of earth, purified seven times." Job 22:25, "... God Almighty will be thy defence and you shalt have plenty of silver."

> Taste of Gold – (Heavy, thick metal tasting) Valued, Vessels of Gold, Prosperity and riches; II Timothy 2:20, "But in a great house there are not only vessels of gold and...."

Mouth
Bad Breath

> Anger and Revenge. Causes bowels to backup. Can be from relationships or situations not worked out.

Lips

> Looks like they have a smirk, corner of lips curl - spirit of conniving or manipulation.

Jaw

> Tightening up – Controlling Spirit, doing things their own way. Psalms 32:9, "Be ye not as the horse, or the mule, which have no understanding: whose mouth must be held in with bit and bridle, lest they come near unto thee." The revelation of what the Word of God is saying in this Psalm is we don't need to do things our way and wait until something bad happens to call upon the Lord.

> TMJ – brought on by anger and/or controlling spirit.

> Hurting or aching jaw – symbolic of gossiping or a person who likes to talk too much.

Proverbs 10:19, "In the multitude of words there wanteth not sin; but he that refraineth his lips is wise."

Lump in Throat

Fear. Not fully trusting God working in your life.

Neck

Stiffnecked; don't want to be obedient; wanting to do things their way. Exodus 33:5, II Kings 17:14, "Notwithstanding, they would not hear, but hardened their necks, like to the neck of their fathers, that did not believe in the Lord their God."

Stubbornness, Jeremiah 17:23, "But they obeyed not, neither inclined their ear, but made their neck stiff, that they might not hear, nor receive instruction." (According to I Samuel 15:23; "Stubbornness is as iniquity and idolatry.")

We need to understand the Word of God is showing us if we are stubborn, we have an idol in our hearts.

(Could be your husband, your wife, your kids, etc.)

Pinching on left side of neck (like the jugular vein); this is A spirit called suppressing ministry which is under the strongman of antichrist. (Trying to keep person from entering the call of God.)

Pinching on both sides of the neck is called a spirit of attempting to take Christ's place. This is a root of the strongman of antichrist, when we try to judge things by the law.

Pinching like a yoke locked on right side of neck – holding something against someone because of what they have done –yoke of bondage. Example: When Jacob got the blessing from his father, Isaac, and Esau found out about it. Genesis 27:40, "And by thy sword shalt thou live, and shalt serve thy brother; and it shall come to pass when thou shalt have the dominion, that thou shalt break his yoke from off thy neck."

Feeling a thick strong yoke around your neck – from not serving the Lord God Almighty with joyfulness and gladness. Read: Deuteronomy 28:47, 48.

Spine

Pain or Pressure on the top of the spine means the antichrist spirit is locked on and trying to control that person. When ministering to a woman I felt the pressure didn't want to leave the top of the spine...It was because they were opposing a man and woman of God, which is a root of the strongman of the antichrist spirit. As I prayed for her, I kept my hand on it till it left and as I did that, the conviction from the Spirit of the Lord came upon her and another woman and they came clean, confessing their faults.

If you feel the pain or pressure running down the spine, it is because something that happened in the past is still controlling their walk and their decisions for the Lord.

Shoulders

Antichrist spirit – Heavy Pressure resting on shoulders is from trying to bear the burdens of people. Proverbs 12:25, "Heaviness in the heart of man maketh it stoop." Isaiah 9:6, "For unto us a child is born, unto us a son is given: and the government shall be upon His shoulder.", not on our shoulders.

A spirit of heaviness comes in when we try to bear burdens. Notice the Word of God does not say cast your cares on each other. I Peter 5:7, "Casting all your care upon him: for he careth for you."

Pain in one shoulder – Person has a chip on their shoulder—trying to blame everyone else.

Pain in the back (near left shoulder blade) –Someone going against you, usually a family member.

Collar Bone

> Right Collar Bone – Homosexual spirit on a man, also woman hating spirit. I John 4:20, "If a man say, I love God, and hateth his brother, he is a liar: for he that loveth not his brother whom he hath seen, how can he love God whom he hath not seen?"

> Left Collar Bone – Lesbian spirit, also a man hating spirit. (I John 4:20)

Heartburn

> Fear. Stress, Worry. Not being able to just let go.

Chest

> Pressure on center of chest (feels like something is sitting on your chest) sometimes hard to breath – spirit of perversion – sometimes brought in by pornography. (Even if someone else in your household is dabbling in it.)

> Pain in chest with shortness of breath, also brought by a spirit of fear – anxiety attack. II Timothy 1:7, "For God hath not given us the spirit of fear; but of power, and of love, and of a sound mind."

> Pain in Center of Chest feels like it wants to break you in two – Destroyer Demon, Destruction – wants to destroy individual or ministry.

> (Hormah – Numbers 21:3, Exodus 12:23,)

Breast

> Sore or Hurting — Bad milk; in other words, Wrong teaching. When going to a conference in Georgia, my breast kept hurting me. The Lord revealed to me that they were teaching their people, "Once saved, Always saved." There was a woman there who did not want to forgive her husband and she thought she was going to heaven. Matt. 6:14, "For if ye forgive not men their trespasses, neither will your Father

forgive your trespasses." If we die in our sins, we will not go to heaven. Ezekiel 3:20, Hebrews 6:4-6, Revelations 2:6, 3:5, 3:11, 22:19, and II Peter 2:20, 21.

Right Arm

Pain or Pull of the Right Arm – Someone trying to take or pull you out of your rightful position.

Example: When Adonijah, Solomon's brother tried to take the kingdom from Solomon.

I Kings 2:15, "And he said, Thou knowest that the kingdom was mine, and that all Israel set their faces on me, that I should reign: howbeit the kingdom is turned about, and is become my brother's: for it was his from the Lord."

Pain in the arm (I feel it in the right arm) – A pastor not tending to his flock. Zechariah 11:17, "Woe to the idol shepherd that leaveth the flock! The sword shall be upon his arm, and upon his right eye: his arm shall be clean dried up, and his right eye shall be utterly darkened."

Left Arm

Someone coming against you. Example: When Joab came against Amasa and with his right hand he grabbed his beard but in his left arm he took the sword and smote Amasa. (II Samuel 20:9, 10)

Elbow

In the wrong place physically, could even be the wrong spiritual covering over you. Also, could be because someone has been trying to nudge you to get your attention to go the right way of the Lord.

Hand

Hurting or dull pain. Making a vow to God and not keeping it. God says He will destroy all the works of thy hands. Ecclesiastes 5:6, "Suffer not thy mouth to cause thy flesh to sin; neither say thou before the angel, that it was an error: wherefore should God be angry at thy voice, and destroy the work of thine hands?"

Right Hand — represents ordained – developed ministry.

Left Hand — represents ministry not yet developed but called to.

Cold Hands — Spirit of Death.

Palm of the hand aching – problem giving and receiving – could be related to tithing.

Sharp jab on the top of the hand – someone directly affecting you from completely stepping into your call in the five-fold ministry.

*Arthritis in the hands or joints is from Envy and Bitterness. Proverbs 14:30, "A sound heart is the life of the flesh: but envy the rottenness of the bones.

Wrist

Sensing like a handcuff on the wrist, someone trying to keep you in bondage.

Wrist hurting; quick to judge and judging by the law and not by grace and truth. (Like having used a mallot in your hand.)

Fingers

The Fingers in the Left Hand Represent the Office God is calling you for. The Fingers in the Right Hand Represents ordained in front of God and man.

Example: The Thumb - represents the Apostolic Calling.

The Index finger- represents the Prophetic Calling.

The Long finger- represents the Evangelistic calling.

The Ring finger- represents the Pastoral calling.

The Little finger- represents the Teacher calling.

The Five-Fold is mentioned in Ephesians 4:11. When you are feeling pain in any of those fingers in the left hand, it is because that person is not stepping into the call God has for their life. If it is a tingling feeling in the left hand, God is showing you this is the calling He has for their life. When you are feeling pain in any of those fingers in the right hand it is because in some way that person is not walking correctly in the Office God has given them.

Cold Finger Tips — Means Dead Works.

James 2:20 says, "But wilt thou know, O vain man, that faith without works is dead?"

Fingernails

Biting nails comes from Fear, nervousness, and insecurity

Skin

Itching; this comes from the spirit of lust; whether it be the lust of the eyes or the lust of the flesh.

I John 2:16, "For all that is in the world, the lust of the flesh, and the lust of the eyes, and the pride of life, is not of the Father, but is of the world."

Kidneys

Hurting or dull pain in middle lower back (kidneys are a filtering system for the body) – Don't know how to rightly divide the word of God. Still going by our old ways. Jeremiah 6:16, "Thus saith the Lord, Stand ye in the ways, and see, and ask for the old paths, where is the good way, and walk therein and ye shall find rest for your souls."

Stomach

Jab in stomach – just below the ribs –spirit of offence – II Samuel 2; Like what Joab carried against Abner, the captain of King Saul's host; Abner had killed Joab's brother, Asahel. Joab carried the spirit of offence II Samuel 2:26 until, II Samuel 3:27; Joab smote Abner under the fifth rib. We need to remember that offence is not of God. The disciples told Jesus in Matthew 15:12-14, "Then came his disciples, and said unto him, knowest thou that the Pharisees were offended, after they heard this saying? But he answered and said, "Every plant, which my heavenly Father hath not planted, shall be rooted up. Let them alone: they be blind leaders of the blind. And if the blind lead the blind, both shall fall into the ditch." So, if you are getting offended, you have a religious spirit and you are being a Pharisee.

Feels like a dart or darts coming at you in your spirit. – Some one speaking to you or about you adversely. John 7:38 says, "He that believeth on me, as the scripture hath said, out of his belly shall flow rivers of living water." – So, our spirit man dwells in our belly. Proverbs 12:18, "There is that speaketh like the piercings of a sword: but the tongue of the wise is health."

Feeling your stomach upset or queasy is from bitterness. When ministering I either feel it or I see it in the realm of the spirit as a big ball of bitterness. When in a church ministering God had given a woman a beautiful prophetic word for her life but God also showed how she had this big ball of bitterness toward a Leader in the church. In order for God to fulfill the prophetic word she had received, she had to get rid of the bitterness; she began weeping knowing it was true.

Overweight

Feeling bloated or heavy or visually seeing that the person is heavy or overweight physically. Carrying extra weight comes from insecurity and or a spirit of rejection which can cause a person to turn to food for comfort. Jesus said 'I am the bread of life: he that cometh to me shall never hunger; and he that believeth on me shall never thirst." (John 6:35) thirst." (John 6:35)

Feeling like your belly is swollen can also be from a spirit of adultery. (Not confessed or repented of) Number 5:20, 21, "But if thou hast gone aside to another instead of thy husband, and if thou be defiled, and some man have lain with thee beside thine husband: then the priest shall charge the woman with an oath of cursing, and the priest shall say unto the woman, The Lord make thee a curse an oath among thy people, when the Lord doth make thy thigh to rot, and thy belly to swell." The person can actually, in the physical, have an enlarged belly because of the spirit of adultery.

Female Organs

Repressed anger or going against the things of God. In II Samuel 6 when King David brought the Ark of God back into Jerusalem, he danced for 18 miles worshipping Jehovah God girded with a linen ephod and when his wife, Michal Saul's daughter saw this she despised him in her heart; Read verse 16. And because of this Michal had no child; II Samuel 6:23, "Therefore Michal the daughter of Saul had no child unto the day of her death." She became a babysitter for her sister, Merab's 5 kids. II Samuel 21:8.

Feeling of pain or jab in left ovary – comes from not producing fruit. Having a religious spirit - example: Going to church everyday!

A painful stabbing in the private area – masochist spirit.

Upper Back

Near inside of shoulder blade – usually on left side - Feels like a stab- sister, brother, or family member that has something against you. Usually biological family, but it could be brothers and sisters in Christ. Psalm 64:4, "That they may shoot in secret at the perfect: suddenly do they shoot at him and fear not."

Lower Back

Lower Back pain – Unforgiveness settled in. Also, check by having a person sit down or lay down to see if one leg is longer than the other; sometimes we have carried things for so long it affects our stature. Psalms 32:3, 4, "When I kept silence, my bones waxed old through my roaring all the day long. For day and night thy hand was heavy upon me:....' Allow God to use you in the miracle anointing for that person's leg to be restored to the same length. When you go against God it will affect your stature, even your physical height, you will be shorter.

Hips

Hips Hurting is a witchcraft spirit. Example of in a church in Arizona: While ministering my hips were hurting so bad I had to lean up against a table. I heard in the spirit that it was witchcraft. However, I was still waiting for the Lord to reveal where and how it had come in. The Lord revealed it when the Pastor showed us a little sachet that she received from someone who called themselves a Prophet. They said the sachet had money in it and by keeping this with them it would bring finances to them.

People of God, this is witchcraft. Deut. 8:18 says that God gives us the power to have wealth. "But thou shalt remember the Lord thy God: for it is he that giveth thee power to get wealth, that he may establish his covenant which he sware unto thy fathers, as it is this day." God also promises in Malachi 3:8-12 that when we pay our tithes we will be blessed and He will destroy the devourer in our lives.

Loins

Pain in Loins – affecting the lower back and possibly the disc in back because of unforgiveness from childhood toward father. (Father had beaten kids, etc. – unforgiveness settled in loins.)

Knees Hurting

Walk with the Lord is being affected. Doing things that are against the will of God; knowing the truth and aparting from it. Deuteronomy 28:35, "The Lord shall smite thee in the knees, and in the legs."

There was an incident at the airport where the Lord revealed to me, a young man, who worked at Starbucks and was playing around with his spiritual life. His knees began to shake and buckle under as I stood in front of him because of the anointing of the Lord in my life. As I spoke the Word of the Lord to him, God began revealing his heart so that he could get his life right with Our Lord Jesus.

Same as when Belshazzar, the king, in the book of Daniel 5:1-6, when he was going against God and drinking wine out of the gold and silver vessels taken from the temple in Jerusalem. The writing on the wall came to declare judgment and in verse 6 shows Belshazzar's "knees smote one against another." God Almighty wants us to be so full of the Word of God that Deuteronomy 28:10 will be fulfilled; "And all people of the earth shall see that thou art called by the name of the Lord; and they shall be afraid of thee." Fearing the Jesus in your life and coming clean with God.

Feeble or weak feeling in the knees is from lack of strength. Not enough of the Word of God in them and, or no one spiritually supporting them.

Job 4:4 says, "Thy words have upholden him that was falling, and thou hast strengthened the weak knees."

Shins

Sharp pain in the shin, feels like someone just kicked you in the shins. Someone close to you has just undermined you. Example: A Pastor had gone away and left a co-pastor (which by the way, a co-pastor is not biblical; read Ephesians 4:11) in charge and the co-pastor began to direct the people in a different direction—the church had a big split. As we began to minister to the Pastor, I felt the Word of Knowledge as if someone had just kicked me in the shin.

Back of Legs

Pain in the back of legs; striving too hard, need to learn how to follow the leading of the Holy Spirit.

Ankles

Shaky, weak feeling; instability, wavering. The bible says that God does not bless someone who wavers. James 1:6, 7, "But let him ask in faith, nothing wavering. For he that wavereth is like awave of the sea driven with the wind and tossed. For let not that man think that he shall recieve any thing of the Lord."

Toes – Big Toe

Sensation in Big toe on right foot; God wanting that person to be consecrated for Him. Leviticus 8:23, 24, "And he slew it; and Moses took of the blood of it, and put it upon the tip of Aaron's right ear, and upon the thumb of his right hands, and upon the great toe of his right foot."

Big toes hurting, because of going against God. Judges 1:6, 7; The tribe of Judah fought against the enemies of the Israelites and when they captured them they cut off their big toes.

Numbness in Big Toe — Balance with the things of God; understanding and applying God's ways to our lives.

Spasms in toes – like having a charley horse comes from wrong doctrine affecting your walk. (Romans 16:17)

Foot

The underside of the foot hurting; curses of the land need to be broken. Feeling of Heat in bottom of your feet – A sign of traveling in your future.

Bruised Heel – Just underwent an attack of the enemy. Genesis 3:15, "And I will put enmity between thee and the woman, and between thy seed and her seed; it shall bruise thy head and thou shalt bruise his heel."

Different Smells—Aromas and Odors

Smell of Fresh Baked Bread

The Freshness of the Word of God. John 6:35, "And Jesus said unto them, I am the bread of life, he that cometh to me shall never hunger."

Smell of Honey

The Revelation of the Word of God coming forward. – I Samuel 14:26, 27 – When Jonathon dipped his rod in the honey and ate of it his eyes were enlightened.

Smell of Oil

Healing Power in that place. Matthew 25:3, 4 – Virgins that had oil were full of the Holy Spirit.

Smell of a Man's Cologne

One day while I was in my room prostrate upon the floor, praying to the Lord, I clearly smelled a strong wonderful scent of a man's cologne. As I lifted my head, I thought maybe it was a scent coming from the pillow that my head was on, but it wasn't. So, I went back to praying. Then a few minutes went by and again I smelled the same scent. It was the presence of the Lord...my thought was then of how Jesus came as the Son of Man. (Matthew 9:6) When I shared it with my husband, who had been in the other room praying as well, he said he had also smelled the presence of the Lord.

Smell of Rain

Favor of God - Proverbs 16:15 – "....and his favour is a cloud to the latter rain." Zechariah 10:1, "Ask ye of the Lord rain in the time of the latter rain, so the Lord shall make bright clouds, and give them showers of rain, to every one grass in the field." Prosperity, fruit from your labor; (James 5:7). Latter rain will be greater than the former.

Smell of Flowers

While worshipping the Lord, I have smelled the different fragrances of flowers. God is showing us His Presence is with us.

Roses

Song of Solomon 2:1; "I am the rose of Sharon, and the Lily of the valleys." It's the beauty of the Body of Christ.

Smell of Fuller's Soap

Malachi 3:2, God's purging of the old, getting rid of wickedness. Mark 9:3.

Smell of Sex

On several occasions while we were ministering, I have smelt the scent of sex. In some of these cases it was because someone had or was sexually violating the person.

On a trip to the Florida Keys, we stopped along the roadside. When we stepped outside of the vehicle, it smelled like male sperm. It was the spirit of homosexuality in that area.

During praise and worship in a church, I passed in front of a woman. When passing her, I smelt the scent of sex and then I heard in my spirit that she was in fornication. Later, when ministering to her, she confessed she was living with someone and got her life right with the Lord.

Smell of Sulfur

Brimstone is another name for sulfur and is mentioned in the Word of God in Genesis 19:24. When God rained upon Sodom and Gomorrah brimstone and fire. Again in Psalm 11:6, "Upon the wicked he shall rain snare, fire, and brimstone." Also, in Revelation 9:17,

Revelation 14:10 and Revelation 20:10; when the devil is going to be cast into the lake of fire and brimstone, where the beast and the false prophet are, and shall be tormented day and night for ever and ever. When I have smelt this, God showed me that the individual we were ministering to was on a path leading to destruction. (Hell) Another time was when we walked into a church to minister and the Lord revealed that they were not teaching the truth of the Word of God.

Importance of the Seer (Prophetic) Anointing for Healing

Many physical ailments and infirmities are onset by anger, unforgiveness, bitterness, and resentment if they are held on to; yet, not all. We also need to realize that we are the temple of God. When the Holy Spirit comes in and we defile that temple, we are also inviting sickness and infirmities into our bodies. I Corinthians 3:16, 17, "Know ye not that ye are the temple of God, and that the Spirit of God dwelleth in you? If any man defile the temple of God, him shall God destroy, for the temple of God is holy, which temple ye are." We can defile ourselves through sexual sin, adultery, fornication, homosexuality, by drugs, alcohol, smoking etc. In this section, we will go over what the Word of God says in regards to infirmities and sicknesses. According to the Word of God in Exodus 15:26, "And said, If thou wilt diligently hearken to the voice of the Lord thy God, and wilt do that which is right in his sight, and wilt give ear to his commandments, and keep all his statutes, I will put none of these diseases upon thee, which I have brought upon the Egyptians: for I am the Lord that healeth thee." You notice by this scripture and many other scriptures throughout the Bible that God says "If, Then." So, you see the "If" is up to us, and "Then," God will do what He said. However, not all sicknesses are from us opening the door to the enemy. If you recall, when the disciples asked Jesus in John 9:2, "And his disciples asked him, saying, Master, who did sin, this man or his parents, that he was born blind?" You may be wondering why the disciples would ask this question. First of all, how can a baby sin when they are just born? I believe the disciples were so confounded by what had just happened in John 8, where the Pharisees had brought the woman found in adultery to Him. Jesus spoke direct to the Pharisees letting them know that God was not their Father and they were going to hell and in the last two verses of John 8 the Pharisees picked up stones to cast at Jesus. The disciples didn't really think about what they were saying. However, the disciples knew the law according to Deuteronomy 5:9, "Thou shalt not bow down thyself unto them, nor serve them, for I, the Lord thy God, am a jealous God, visiting the iniquity of the fathers upon the children unto the third and fourth generation of them that hate me." Understanding the ways of Our God is very important. If we are still trying to follow Jesus Christ by the law, we are submitting ourselves under the judgments of the law. Unless we repent, this can affect our children. Jesus said to the Pharisees, the religious folks, because you submit yourself to the law, you will be judged by the law. John 5:45 says, "Do not think that I will accuse you to the Father; there is one that accuseth you, even Moses, in whom ye trust." If you read Romans chapter 7 carefully, you will understand the Apostle Paul is saying that as long as we are married to the law, we are committing spiritual adultery. If we are married to the law we cannot be married to the Grace, which is Jesus Christ. Now, let's look at what Jesus' reply was as to why this man was born blind; John 9:3, "Jesus answered, "Neither hath this man sinned, nor his parents; but that the works of God should be manifest in him." So you see, this was all for the Glory of the Lord. Another example of an infirmity and sickness that was all for the Glory of the Lord was in John 11:1-46, Lazarus was sick and Lazaruss' sisters had sent for Jesus so He could come pray for their brother so that he would be healed. Look at the Bigness of Our God. John 11:4; "When Jesus heard that, he said, "This sickness is not unto death, but for the Glory of God, that the Son of God might be glorified thereby." Having said this, verse 6 shows us that Jesus waited another 2 days before He went to go see Lazarus. Now remember, Jesus had just said this was not a sickness unto death and yet Lazarus was dead when He got there. This is because of the Bigness of Our God. Knowing all things, Jesus knew that He was going to show them that He is Our Resurrection, Power, and Life and that by Him we live and breathe and have our being. By following Jesus, we shall not die spiritually but have eternal life. We see now that sickness can come in by us opening a door for the enemy, by generational curses if we are still under the law, and some sicknesses are for God's Glory. There is also another reason as the Word of God says in Hebrews 9:27, "And as it is appointed unto men once to die, but after this the judgment." Unless we are going home with the Lord at the time of rapture, there will be a time for our physical bodies to die. There are two more scriptures I want to bring to your attention that affect your life span. The first, Ephesians 6:1-3, "Children, obey your parents in the Lord: for this is right. Honour thy father and mother; (which is the first commandment with promise;) that it may be well with thee, and thou mayest live long on the earth." The second, when we take the last supper and we know that we haven't gotten right with one another and with God, we are inviting sickness and possibly death into our lives. I Corinthians 11:29, 30, "For he that eateth and drinketh unworthily, eateth and drinketh damnation to himself, not discerning the Lord's body. For this cause many are weak and sickly among you, and many sleep."

Below is a list of infirmities and sickness and possible causes of these sicknesses. Remember, having that relationship with the Holy Spirit and knowing His voice when you are ministering deliverance to someone is of utmost importance. The secrets of their hearts will be revealed so they can receive their deliverance and their healing. As you read these different aliments and infirmities, remember to only use these as a guideline for there could be many other reasons or causes.

Abdominal cramps

> Holding on to something. Let it go and give it to God. (Some women refer to it as PMS).

Abscess Tooth

> Envy and Bitterness have set in. Proverbs 14:30.

Acne

> Rejection and insecurity.

Addictions

> Not wanting to confront or feeling they're not able to confront; therefore, turning to something for comfort.

Addisons' disease

> Living by their emotions instead of in the spirit.

Adrenal glands

> Holds things in, problem releasing things. Feelings of Defeat.

AIDS

> Immune system destroyed from going against the ways of God or not allowing Jesus Christ to be all in all in your life.

Alcoholism

> Same as addictions, Self rejection and hatred.

Allergies

> Immune system weakened; person not strong in the Word of God.

Alzheimers

> Feeling defeated, helpless.

Amnesia

> Fear that entered in from a traumatic incident that happened in the past.

Anemia

> Spirit of Justification. "Yes-but" answer to things especially to correction.

Ankles

> Problems with the Achilles heel or the Achilles tendon due to a weak spot or area in our walk with the Lord.

Anorexia

> Self Rejection. Self Hatred. Fear of Failure. Fear of Future. Fear of Man – people pleasing spirit.

Anxiety

> Anxiety attacks are brought on by the spirit of fear. Not fully trusting in the Lord. Focused on the situation and not on Jesus.

Appendicitis

> Holding on to things, not knowing how to release things without anger. Stress from deadlines.

Appetite

> Overeating — Insecurity, looking for comfort. Under eating — Self Rejection, Self Hatred. Same as anorexia.

Arteries

> Clogged — Not allowing God to use you for His Glory.

Arthritis

> Bitterness, resentment and feeling unloved.

Asthma

> Smothering Love, feeling unable to do for self because someone else is always trying to do things for you.

Athletes Foot

> Feeling unaccepted, Frustrated with your situation.

Back

> Lower – unforgiveness, not letting go of the past.

> Middle – Handling matters your way instead of God's way.

> Upper - Trying to carry your burdens.

Bad Breath

> Halitosis - Anger and Revenge, usually backs up your bowels giving your breath a foul odor.

Balance

> Equilibrium – Not rightly dividing the Word of God when it comes to your life; which brings opposing forces.

Baldness

> Tension from trying to control things and fear of losing control. Also, from having a haughty spirit thinking we can do whatever we want and thinking God doesn't judge it. Read Isaiah 3:24, "And it shall come to pass, that instead of sweet smell there shall be stink; and instead of a girdle a rent; and instead of well set hair baldness; and instead of a stomacher a girding of sackcloth; and burning instead of beauty."

Barren Womb

> Can be from generational curse, read Leviticus 20:20, "And if a man shall lie with his uncle's wife, he hath uncovered his uncle's nakedness: they shall bear their sin; they shall die childless." Also, could be from a spirit of rejection.

Bed wetting

> Fear of your parents, usually fear of your father.

Belching

> Being anxious and in a hurry for things.

Blackheads

> Fear of rejection, and anger.

Bladder

> Weak bladder – not forgiving yourself from the past. Fear of letting go.

Bleeding gums

> Irritations and not wanting to listen to others.

Blindness

> Anger, Hatred – Brings in Blindness to the point that you can't even find your car keys, even if they are right in front of you. I John 2:11, "But he that hateth his brother is in darkness, and walketh in darkness, and knoweth not whither he goeth, because that darkness hath blinded his eyes."

> Lack of brotherly kindness. II Peter 1:7, 8, and 9:

> "… And to godliness brotherly kindness; and to brotherly kindness charity. For if these things be in you, and abound, they make you that you shall neither be barren nor unfruitful in the knowledge of our Lord Jesus Christ. But he that lacketh these things is blind, and cannot see afar off, and hath forgotten that he was purged from his old sins."

Blood Pressure

> High – Hypertension; not resolving problems from relationships in the past.

> Low — Feeling Defeated – lack of love as a child.

Body Odor

> Fear of others liking you. Remember we are here to please God. Galatians 1:10, "For do I now persuade men, or God? Or do I seek to please men? For if I yet pleased men, I should not be the servant of Christ."

Boils

> Anger brought on by rejection.

Bone Marrow

> Problems in the family or feeling like you don't fit in.

Breast

> Lumps and Cysts - Trying to overprotect or having an overbearing attitude toward others.

Breathing Problems

> Such as Hyperventilation – Frustrations, overwhelmed and feelings of too much responsibility.

> Shallow Breathing – Not grasping and getting all that God has for you.

Bronchitis

> Problems in the Family; sometimes a lot of arguing and sometimes no one talking to each other.

Bruises

> Bruising easily is usually due to letting little things bother you.

Bulimia

> Rejection, usually by family member or members, self hatred, trying to fit in.

Bunions

> Waiting for everyone else to make a stand for the Lord instead of going forward. Not standing as the priest God has called you to be in your home.

Burns

> Feeling like you're the only one doing any work, etc. – being angry and hurt, feeling sorry for yourself.

Callous

> Insensitive, hardened due to the trials and tribulations in life.

Cancer

Unforgiveness, and hurt toward someone in the past.

Candida

Suspicious and lack of trust in relationship; causing frustration. Being a very demanding person at times. Same as yeast infection.

Canker Sores

Blaming others and not knowing how to stand up for self. Festering up from resentment and bitterness.

Car Sickness

Fear and concentrating on self instead of others. Not being in control. Same as: Motion Sickness.

Carpal-Tunnel

Syndrome

Feeling like someone else is getting something over you.

Cataracts

Looking at life through the law instead of thru the spirit.

Cellulite

Stored anger or resistance to giving in.

Circulation

Holds back on things - Unable to express self correctly.

Claustrophobia

Fear of someone closing in on you, fear of losing control.

Colds

> Busyness of life, slow down.

Colitis

> Fear of the Future, not totally releasing the past.

Coma

> Fear, not wanting to go on. A means of escape from their situations.

Conjunctivitis

> Pink eye — The things of this life have you entangled.

Constipation

> Backed up from refusing to let things go.

Corns

> Tender areas in your life. The enemy knows just where to push your button.

Cramps

> (See abdominal cramps.)

Deafness

> Stubbornness and feeling rejected.

Dementia

> See Alzheimers.

Depression

> Sets in when we have repressed anger and we don't know how to confront the situation or person.

Diabetes

> Having uncertainty of the future, fear of losing control.

Diarrhea

> Trying to deal with things on your own.

Dizziness

> Vertigo - Not wanting to deal with or handle situations.

Earache

> Not listening to God, rebellion to the voice of God.

Emphysema

> Fear of the Future, feeling unworthy.

Epilepsy

> Sometimes from something traumatic that happened to them in the past. Hurts to remember.

Eye Problems

> Nearsighted — Fear of the Future.

> Farsighted — Fear of taking a closer look at things.

Fainting

> Unable to cope with things.

Foot Problems

> Not taking heed to the Word of God; King Asa in II Chronicles 16:12 was diseased in his feet because he did not want to heed to what the Prophet said.

Frigid

> Insecurity and fear of failure.

Fungus

> On toes or under fingernails, caused by old ways; such as family traditions. Jeremiah 9:14 says, "But have walked after the imagination of their own heart, and after Baalim, which their fathers taught them."

Gallbladder

> Problems with gallbladder and/or gallstones enters when we are stubborn to do the things that God is telling us; instead we want to do it our way.

Gangrene

> Not living for the Lord, blood flow begins to become inhibited.

Gas

> Flatulence and/or pain in the intestines from gas – Fear from incompletion of matters.

Glands

> Wanting others to do for you what you should be doing for yourself.

Goiter

> Feeling controlled and stopped from doing what they want to do.

Gout

> Dominating attitude, becoming impatient and angry. (Or that person even being dominated by someone.)

Grey hair

> Anxiety, stress, and abnormal amount of pressure.

Gum disease

> Feeling trapped, unable to get out of rut.

Headaches

> Rebellion toward authority.

Heart Attack

> Brought on by caring more for the things of the world than the things of God.

Heartburn

> Worry, anxiety, fear of the unknown.

Hemorrhoids

> Stressing about many issues; afraid to let others handle matters.

Hepatitis

> Liver problems – filtering system; unable to rightly apply the Word of God for our own situations.

Hernia

> Broken or severed relationship with someone very close and dear to them.

Herpes

> Sexual guilt; feeling they need to be punished for their actions.

Hip Problems

> Problems going forward in the Lord, due to self and/or others. Also, could be a spirit of witchcraft, which is a control spirit.

Hives

> Tormenting spirit – not fully forgiving someone.

Hodgkins Disease

> Fear of not being good enough; always trying to prove self and get to the top.

Hunchback

> Humpback – always trying to be there for others; carrying others burdens.

Hyperactivity

> Anxiety, Fear – trying to please others.

Hyperventilation

> Frustrated and overwhelmed; feeling as though too much responsibility has been put on them.

Impotence

> Insecurity in sexual performance – feeling belittled or ridiculed.

Indigestion

> Not accepting things and/or not wanting to accept responsibility. Fear, anxiety.

Infection

> Easily offended, angry and irritated.

Influenza

> Believing on and accepting ways other than God's ways.

Ingrown nail

> Brought on by guilt and shame; not able to go forward easily.

Insanity

> Unable to cope with things; escape, withdrawal.

Itching

> Sometimes this is from lust; itching for things, wanting change, not satisfied.

Jaw

> Tightened jaw. TMJ – brought on by anger, unable to cope with and/or confront.

Joints

> Doesn't like change. Resistant.

Kidney

> Old ways of thinking; not accepting what the Spirit is saying. Not being able to rightly filter (divide) the Word of God.

Knee

> Their walk with God is not good. Deuteronomy 28:35 says, that if we do not heed to the Word of God that "The Lord shall smite thee in the knees, and in the legs...."

Laryngitis

> Fearful and scared to say what you think; feeling that when you do speak it is not always received.

Leukemia

> Hopelessness. Sometimes brought in by family not letting go of the past.

Lou Gehrig's

Disease

> Not doing things for God's glory; looking for approval of man instead of God.

Liver

Does not easily accept correction. Stubborn, set in their ways.

Lung

Allowing someone or something to suck the life out of you. Insecure.

Lupus

Sometimes from being mistreated as child, person gives up. Suppressed anger.

Menopause

Problems

Fear of aging, fear of being rejected, or feelings of not being wanted. Remember, Jesus says in Hebrews 13:5, "I will never leave thee, nor forsake thee." The true Fountain of Youth is Jesus Christ, the "Living Water."

Migraine

Headaches are usually from rebellion. When it comes to migraines, it can also include repressed anger and/or not satisfied sexually and unloved.

Miscarriage

Fear of Future, not able to cope with change and/or do not like confrontations. Also, I have seen this affect a whole congregation when they had been praying against principalities in the second heaven.

Mono

Tired of feeling they are the only ones giving. Not caring for self. Feeling sorry for self.

Multiple Sclerosis

A Hardness when evaluating or judging a situation.

Muscular Dystrophy

Not liking responsibility. Giving up.

Nails

Biting or always fidgeting with nails; nervousness, fear of man, and/or never being satisfied.

Neck Problems

Stubborn and stiffnecked. I Samuel 15:23 says, "....and Stubbornness is as iniquity and idolatry." (Husbands, wives, kids, jobs, etc. can be idols in our hearts.)

Nervous Breakdown

Taking everything upon self – not knowing how to release things to the Lord. Self-centered.

Nodules

Frustrated, resenting others for not helping. A lot of times it has to do with a person's job or career. Martha syndrome; Luke 10:40, "But Martha was cumbered about much serving, and came to him, and said, Lord, dost thou not care that my sister hath left me to serve alone? Bid her therefore that she help me."

Nose Bleeds

A lot of times, kids needing attention; wanting to know they are loved. Feeling neglected.

Osteoporosis

Trying to do things in our own strength for a long time. Thinking they do not have support where needed.

Pancreatitis

> Not knowing how to release the frustrations in their life. Holding on to the bad instead of remembering the good things in their lives.

Parasites

> Something or someone trying to control their life. Usually because of a spirit of insecurity.

Plantar Warts

> Bone spurs – when our lives are not balanced with the things of the Lord.

Prostrate

> Prostrate problems usually come in because of fear of aging and harboring bitterness from the past.

Psoriasis

> Having a hate for the authority in the land – such as the police. Romans 13:1-4 – Going against the authority in the land is going against God because God had ordained this.

Rashes

> Impatient, irritated when made to wait.

Rheumatoid Arthritis

> Holding on to grudges. Living in the past.

Rickets

> Lack of Love....family problems usually between the husband and wife.

Linda Morales

Ringworm

> Having an unclean spirit and allowing others to use or control you and staying in that same cycle.

Sciatic Nerve

> Fear of losing money, fear of failure, and fear of the future.

Scoliosis

> Feeling left out; trying to fit in.

Shingles

> Fear and tension – takes things upon themselves.

Sickle Cell

Anemia

> Insecurity, feeling like a failure. Loss of something valuable in their life.

Sinusitis

> Anger and rage backup – usually toward someone they are around a lot or all the time.

Stroke

> Wanting to be cared for and loved. Needing attention. Sometimes just tired of always having been the caretaker.

Stuttering

> Or stammering is from fear of failure, insecurity; having relied on others to do for them.

Sty

> Usually, built up anger; looking on people hypocritically.

Teeth

Grinding

Same as jaw problems; holding on to anger.

Thrush

Occurs in infants, however; could stem from parent/parents getting angry when they make the wrong decisions.

Thyroid Problems

Hyperthyroid – Graves Disease – Impatient, trying to take control but feeling unable.

Hypothyroid – Goiter – Feelings of giving up, Defeat, feeling worthless.

Tinnitis

Search heart for an area not repented of; in I Samuel 3:11; God spoke to Prophet Samuel about judgement coming because of Eli and and the people of Israel not taking heed to God's Word. It says, "And the Lord said to Samuel, Behold I will do a thing in Israel at which both ears of every one that heareth it shall tingle." Again, the same reason is shown in II Kings 21:12.

Tonsillitis

Fear of man, fear of saying what needs to be said. Worried about losing something or someone.

Tuberculosis

Life being destroyed because of self-centeredness and being very possessive.

Tumors

Idols in our hearts. I Samuel 5:6, "But the hand of the Lord was heavy upon them of Ashdod, and he destroyed them, and smote them with emerods, even Ashdod and the coast thereof."

Holding on to old hurts; letting these old hurts affect your judgment and going forward.

Ulcers

Taking what people say to them too seriously. Letting negative words eat at you!

Varicose Veins

Stressed out, discouraged, feeling like they are in a situation or relationship they don't like but don't know how to resolve.

Vertigo

Same as dizziness, feeling confused and not knowing which way to turn.

Yeast

Infection

Same as Candida; wanting to be in control, demanding.

VISIONS AND DREAMS

God uses many symbols to illustrate to us what is going on, whether it is for ourselves, for another individual, for the Body of Christ, or for a nation. Jesus spoke in parables to the disciples and in most cases the way He spoke was like a picture you could visualize. There are several reasons why He spoke in parables. One reason is that when the Scribes and Pharisees blasphemed against the Holy Spirit saying in Mark 3:22 that Jesus cast out devils by the prince of devils. In Mark 3:30 they said that Jesus had an unclean spirit. Jesus did not speak, except in parables, from that time forward because blaspheming against the Holy Spirit is an unpardonable sin according to Mark 3:29. The revelation behind Mark 4:11, 12, "And he said unto them, Unto you it is given to know the mystery of the kingdom of God: but unto them that are without, all these things are done in parables: that seeing they may see, and not perceive, and hearing they may hear, and not understand; lest at any time they should be converted, and their sins should be forgiven them." God does not change His Word for any of us so when someone blasphemes against the Holy Spirit, God closes their understanding. When God speaks to us through parables, or visions, or dreams, He also will reveal and give us the understanding of these mysteries as He has spoken in Ephesians 3:1-5. As the saying goes, "a picture paints a thousand words;" many revelations can come forward and we can remember and apply them easier by being able to visualize it. In other words, thru visions and dreams God can speak many things to us.

We need to learn to communicate with the Holy Spirit to understand what God is trying to show us. Remember the Holy Spirit is the third person of the Trinity. The Prophet Elijah was crying out to God and he wanted God to answer him. I Kings 19:10-13, "And he said, I have been very jealous for the Lord God of hosts: for the children of Israel have forsaken thy covenant, thrown down thine altars, and slain thy prophets with the sword; and I, even I only, am left; and they seek my life to take it away. And he said, Go forth, and stand upon the mount before the Lord. And behold, the Lord passed by, and a great and strong wind rent the mountains, and brake in pieces the rocks before the Lord; but the Lord was not in the wind: and after the wind an earthquake; but the Lord was not in the earthquake: and after the earthquake a fire; but the Lord was not in the fire: and after the fire a still small voice. And it was so when Elijah heard it, that he wrapped his face in his mantle, and went out, and stood in the entering in of the cave. And behold, there came a voice unto him and said, "What doest thou here, Elijah?" Jehovah God, Our Father, Jesus Christ, the True God, loves to answer prayer when we are seeking Him. However, God answers in His Way. I believe many of us have been or are like the Prophet Elijah wanting God to answer us in some spectacular way. As you notice, Prophet Elijah thought he was the only one left serving God but God told him in verse 18 that He had 7,000 others that had not bowed down to Baal. God truly has a sense of humor. First came the strong wind that rent the mountains, then the earthquake that shook the earth, and then came the flaming fire. It wasn't until everything was calm that God Spoke In the Still Small Voice. And in that you'll notice that the Prophet Elijah had to hide his face in his mantle and go out of the cave and then God spoke to him. I believe Prophet Elijah realized that God was saying… "Hey, just let me be God." Psalm 46:10 says, "Be still, and know that I am God…" The Holy Spirit is the still small voice. In other words, being in tune with the Spirit of the Living God within us.

Something very important the Lord showed me, whether it is a vision, a dream, or a voice, we should always ask the Lord if this is from Him. When a person is very busy or worried they may have many dreams but these dreams are not from the Lord. My husband will ask the person, "You been eatin' a lot of pizza?" Ecclesiastes 5:3, "For a dream cometh through the multitude of business; and a fool's voice is known by multitude of words." After you go through deliverance you may have what we call cleansing dreams where the old is being taken out and God replacing the new. (Such as in the depth of our subconscious.) Job 33:14-17, "For God speaketh once, yea twice, yet man perceiveth it not. In a dream, in a vision of the night, when deep sleep falleth upon men, in slumberings upon the bed; then he openeth the ears of men, and sealeth their instruction, that he may withdraw man from his purpose, and hide pride from man." God gives us these dreams and visions to show what has happened, what is happening, or what is going to happen. Always test the spirit in accordance with I John 4:1-3 and as explained in the previous section of this book, Understanding the Spiritual Realm. Whether it is a vision, a dream, or a voice, it should not go against the word of God. James 3:17, "But the wisdom that is from above is first pure, then peaceable, gentle, and easy to be entreated, full of mercy and good fruits, without partiality, and without hypocrisy. And the fruit of righteousness is sown in peace of them that make peace." Any bitterness, strife, envying or lies is not from the Lord. James 3:15, 16 says, "This wisdom descendeth not from above, but is earthly, sensual, devilish. For where envying and strife is, there is confusion and every evil work."

Remember confusion is not from God. An example of this, something not from God, is found in I Samuel 28:6-20 when God did not answer King Saul. He went to a woman that had a familiar spirit and asked her to call Prophet Samuel back from the dead. This was not Prophet Samuel; this was a familiar spirit. God is not going to speak through a psychic, through withchcraft, through horoscopes, through a familiar spirit, or through any kind of spirit of divination. Our God is a Holy God! You cannot call someone back from the dead to speak to you. The Bible states clearly, it is appointed for man to die once and then judgment. (Hebrews 9:27) God brings conviction to get right with Him; comfort and edification to go forward in the Lord. God does not put fear of man on us or try to hurt us. Another reason you know this was not of God is because it says Prophet Samuel told King Saul that David would take over his kingdom. God would never say someone else's name to hurt us. So, always test the spirit and know what is from God's Throne and what is not.

Another way God speaks to us is through angels, just like He did throughout the Bible. Genesis 16:7-11 when an angel came to Hagar, Sarai's handmaid, to inform her to return and submit herself. In other words don't listen to your flesh, which is the soulish realm: the mind, will, and the emotions! In Genesis 19:1-22, two deliverance angels came to get Lot and his family out of Sodom and Gomorrah. In John

20:11, 12, Two angels in the sepulchre spoke to Mary as she was in search of the "Lover of Her Soul." Daniel 9:21, 22; the angel, Gabriel, came to give the Prophet skill and understanding. Luke 1:19; the angel, Gabriel, came to Zacharias to bring glad tidings. Acts 10:3-48; an angel came to Cornelius to tell him to send for the Apostle Peter to hear the Good News, Jesus Christ, and to understand the importance of the five-fold ministry. There are many more mentioned throughout the Word of God.

I am going to share a few of the experiences I have had with God's angels. On one occasion, while driving to the airport with one of the Prophets in our ministry, we were running a little late and still needed to pick-up one of the other Prophets going with us. It was around 3:30 in the morning and I let out a shout of joy unto the Lord; and said, "I know in my spirit God is sending us." Less than five minutes passed, and the exit we were to take was closed off for construction. (Remember we were already running late.) I said we don't need to worry let's just go the opposite way and somehow the Lord will show us how to get turned around. We took the next available exit and as we exited the ramp there was an overpass with about five (what appeared to be homeless) people drinking under the overpass. The Prophet with me said, "Hey, Prophet, look the car off to your right; I believe the lady is trying to say something to you." So, I looked to the right and in that car was a beautiful black woman, her countenance flawless and glowing. I rolled down my window and she said unto me, "You want to make a left, then go straight and take the second left." I had not asked her for directions. She told me as she smiled, the most beautiful soft loving smile, where I needed to go to be heading in the right direction. I truly know this was an angel sent of My Lord. Once, in Georgia, I was so exhausted from work, the drive, and then ministering to people, that at about 12 o'clock midnight I went to sleep. My husband stayed up still talking with people. At around 3 or 4 in the morning I felt a distinct tap on my left shoulder, which woke me up. I thought it was my husband until I heard him lightly snoring – ZZZZ-Z. I said, "Lord is it you?" I heard, "Pray." I began to pray in the spirit and as I began praying the angel of the Lord let me know it was for the teenage boy, whose bed we were sleeping in, and began revealing all that he was doing. The next day, it was confirmed that everything was true and repentance came and the young man reconciled with Jesus. Angels "Of the Lord" are different than angels "From the Lord". The angels "Of the Lord" are for us and accomplish the Word of the Lord; Hebrews 1:13, 14 and Psalm 103:20. The fallen angels that went with satan are "From the Lord". I Samuel 16:23: "And it came to pass, when the evil spirit FROM God was upon Saul."

God said in Amos 3:7, "Surely the Lord God will do nothing, but he revealeth his secret unto his servants the prophets. When we are walking in the spirit and seated with Christ in the heavenlies as it says in Ephesians 2:6, "And hath raised us up together and made us sit together in heavenly places in Christ Jesus," God will show us things before they happen. The revelation is when you are seated in the heavenlies with the Master you will be looking down and seeing any plan of the enemy. When God shows us something bad about to happen to someone or even a trap the enemy has for us, we can pray against it. For the word of God says in II Corinthians 10:3, 4, "For though we walk in the flesh, we do not war after the flesh: For the weapons of our warfare are not carnal, but mighty through God to the pulling down of strongholds." So learn how to cancel things out of the spiritual realm. The Word of God says God tempts no man but man is tempted by his own evil desires. Read it in James 5:13, 14, "Let no man say when he is tempted, I am tempted of God, for God cannot be tempted with evil, neither tempteth he any man: But every man is tempted, when he is drawn away of his own lust, and enticed." There are many things that we have put out into the realm of the spirit from our words, our actions, or even our thoughts, before and even after we accepted Jesus Christ into our lives. God will allow these thoughts, words, or even actions to come back around so that we can put them under our feet, if we haven't already. That is why the scripture says in II Corinthians 10:5, 6, "Casting down imaginations, and every high thing that exalteth itself against the knowledge of God, and bringing into captivity every thought to the obedience of Christ; and having in a readiness to revenge all disobedience, when your obedience is fulfilled." Having a readiness to revenge all disobedience means from all that we have put out into the realm of the spirit — wicked thoughts or desires. We need to search our hearts everyday like the Word of God says in Psalms 4:4, "Stand in awe, and sin not: commune with your own heart upon your bed, and be still." As we search our hearts, God reminds us of these thoughts or desires. What we need to do is grab them back from out of the realm of the spirit and repent for them, covering them with the blood of Jesus. That is the way we take revenge on all disobedience. Repentance is the key to walking this life out in the spirit and walking in holiness! Humbling ourselves, so Jesus Christ can be all in all in our lives.

Word of warning for all of us: when the Lord reveals something for you to share or tell someone else, don't say, "the Holy Spirit told me this," or "the Holy Spirit showed me this." It is better to say, "I feel in my spirit," or "I feel the Lord was showing me." We do not want to speak lightly of the Holy Spirit. The Bible says in Matthew 12:31, 32, "Wherefore I say unto you, all manner of sin and blasphemy shall be forgiven unto men: but the blasphemy against the Holy Ghost shall not be forgiven unto men. And whosoever speaketh a word against the Son of man, it shall be forgiven him: but whosoever speaketh against the Holy Ghost, it shall not be forgiven him, neither in this world, neither in the world to come." Let me give you an example in the book of Acts 21:10, 11; There was a Prophet called Agabus. He prophesied to the Apostle Paul saying, "Thus saith the Holy Ghost," that the man whose hands he bound with the girdle would be bound by the Jews and turned over to the Gentiles. You will notice in Acts 21:33; it was not the Jews who bound the Apostle Paul, it was the chief captain and the centurions who bound him. All I am saying, "Is let us not use the Holy Spirit lightly," let us reverence Him.

You may be asking, "What do you mean by visions?" As we establish ourselves in a five-fold ministry, the prophetic anointing, revelations, and the gifts of the Spirit will begin to operate in our lives. The Prophetic anointing will increase because the foundations are established as written in Ephesians 2:20 on the Apostolic and the Prophetic. The Apostle Paul operating in a five-fold ministry in obedience to Christ knew because of that he would be moving in the prophetic and God would be giving him dreams and visions. II Corinthians 12:1, "It is not expedient for me doubtless to glory. I will come to visions and revelations of the Lord." The revelations will begin to come because it says in Ephesians 3:1-5, "For this cause I Paul, the prisoner of Jesus Christ for you Gentiles, If ye have heard of the dispensation of the grace of God which is given me to you-ward: How that by revelation he made known unto me the mystery; (as I wrote afore in few words, Whereby, when ye read, ye may understand my knowledge in the mystery of Christ. Which in other ages was not made known unto the sons of men, as it is now revealed unto his Holy Apostles and Prophets by the Spirit." The gifts of the Spirit as are written in I Corinthians 12:4-12 will begin to increase and manifest within the Body of Christ. The need for God's people moving in the prophetic is so that as the Word of God says in Ezekiel 3:17 that we can be watchmen for God's people, seeing into the hearts (according to I Corinthians 14:25), because the Lord Jesus is looking for a bride without spot or wrinkle or blemish, or any such thing, (Ephesians 5:27)

Visions are divine revelations to the mind of the Prophet. In Psalm 89:19 says the Lord speaks through visions. Also, in Numbers 12:6, 7, 8, "And he said, Hear now my words: If there be a prophet among you, I the Lord will make myself known unto him in a vision, and will speak unto him in a dream. My servant Moses is not so, who is faithful in all mine house. With him will I speak mouth to mouth, even apparently, and not in dark speeches; and the similitude of the Lord shall he behold: wherefore then were ye not afraid to speak against my servant Moses?" God speaks to Prophets through visions and dreams and Moses, representing the Apostolic, God says He speaks mouth to mouth. This means the Apostles will have an encounter with the Lord in the spirit just like the Apostle Paul had in the book of Acts chapter 9 on his way to Damascus. Throughout the Word of God, God spoke to the Prophets through dreams and visions. Through dreams and visions God imparts instruction. (Job 33:14, 16, 17) As mentioned before, when we worry so much or we are so preoccupied with the things of the world, many times when we sleep our minds begin to relax and we have all kinds of crazy dreams that are not from the Lord. The Word of God shows this in Ecclesiastes 5:3. Jeremiah 23:25, 26, says, "I have heard what the prophets said, that prophesy lies in my name, saying, I have dreamed, I have dreamed. How long shall this be in the heart of the prophets that prophesy lies? Yea, they are prophets of the deceit of their own heart." Think about it. Why would God give a dream to someone, who is not spending time in the Word of God or separated for the Lord, regarding someone else? I believe if we are not living for the Lord that God would give us a dream for ourselves, to correct our own lives, but not for someone else. An example of this is in Genesis 20:2-7; Abraham allowed fear in his life and told Abimelech, king of Gerar, Sarah was his sister and God came to Abimelech in a dream. Read it; Genesis 20:2-7,

"And Abraham said of Sarah his wife, she is my sister: and Abimelech king of Gerar sent, and took Sarah. But God came to Abimelech in a dream by night, and said to him, Behold, thou are but a dead man, for the woman which thou hast taken; for she is a man's wife. But Abimelech had not come near her: and he said, Lord, wilt thou slay also a righteous nation? Said he not unto me, She is my sister? And she, even she herself said, He is my brother: in the integrity of my heart and innocency of my hands have I done this. And God said unto him in a dream, Yea, I know that thou didst this in the integrity of thy heart; for I also withheld thee from sinning against me: therefore suffered I thee not to touch her. Now, therefore, restore the man his wife: for he is a prophet, and he shall pray for thee, and thou shalt live: and if thou restore her not, know thou that thou shalt surely die, thou, and all that are thine." Notice even though Abraham said she is my sister, God protects His own; through a dream, a vision or whatever it takes; God protects His own. By us communicating with the Spirit of Truth we can learn to ask, "Is this dream from you, Lord?" Then test the spirit. Even if you hear the dream is not from the Lord, learn to go into the spiritual realm and cancel out anything that the enemy would be trying to bring.

Different Types of Visions

1. Inner Visions — A picture you see in your inner man or spirit man. A supernatural appearance that conveys a revelation. like seeing a photo of something.
2. Open Visions—Your eyes are open as if you are watching a movie screen right in front of you. Isaiah 6:1-4, "In the year that King Uzziah died I saw also the Lord sitting upon a throne, high and lifted up, and his train filled the temple. Above it stood the seraphims: each one had six wings; with twain he covered his face, and with twain he covered his feet, and with twain he did fly. And one cried unto another, and said, Holy, holy, holy, is the Lord of hosts: the whole earth is full of his glory. And the posts of the door moved at the voice of him that cried, and the house was filled with smoke." (I Samuel 3:1, Ezekiel 8:4-6)
3. Night Visions—Night visions are dreams. Job 33:14-17, "For God speaketh once, yea twice, yet man perceiveth it not. In a dream,

in a vision of the night, when deep sleep falleth upon men, in slumberings upon the bed; then he openeth the ears of men, and sealeth their instruction, that he may withdraw man from his purpose, and hide pride from man." Also, in the book of Daniel, God spoke to King Nebuchadnezzar in a dream that he was having a hard time remembering. When the three Hebrew boys interceded for Prophet Daniel and got into the presence of the Lord; God gave the dream and the understanding of the dream to Prophet Daniel. Daniel 2:19, "Then was the secret revealed unto Daniel in a night vision. Then Daniel blessed the God of heaven." The word of the Lord says in Genesis 41:32, if you dream a dream twice it is because God will shortly bring it to pass. Genesis 41:32, "And for that the dream was doubled unto Pharoah twice; it is because the thing is established by God, and God will shortly bring it to pass." Also, when you dream in black and white, most of the time, that is the past; and when you dream in color it shows something that is presently happening or going to happen.

4.   Trance—A trance is your natural abilities being frozen so God can minister to you what is needed. When Peter was on the housetop praying, he went into a trance: Acts 10:10, "And he became very hungry, and would have eaten: but while they made ready, he fell into a trance." In Acts 11:5, Peter was explaining to the other Jews about the trance God put him in revealing that it was not wrong to go to the Gentiles. In Numbers 24:4 the Prophet Balaam was in a trance: "He hath said, which heard the words of God, which saw the vision of the Almighty, falling into a trance, but having his eyes open." Sometimes we think it is ourselves, that we are so tired, when it is the Lord making us that way in order to put instructions within us like Apostle Peter in Acts chapter 10 and Abraham in Genesis chapter 15.

Daniel was an awesome Prophet of God, separated, walking pure before the Lord. God even called Daniel greatly beloved three different times; In Daniel 9:23, Daniel 10:11, and in Daniel 10:19. God had given the Prophet Daniel understanding in all dreams and visions. Daniel 1:17, "As for these four children, God gave them knowledge and skill in all learning and wisdom; and Daniel had understanding in all visions and dreams." I prayed and declared this scripture over my life for about

2 years. The Lord fulfilled it and gives me the understanding in all visions and dreams; All Glory goes to the Lord! Psalms 138:2 says, "I will worship toward thy holy temple, and praise thy name for thy loving kindness and for thy truth: for thou hast magnified thy word, above all thy name." In other words, God honors His Word over His Name; so if we pray the Word back to God for our lives He will honor it. The Word of God says that God's Word will not return void, and by speaking the Word of God over your own life, it will surely come to pass. My husband and I spoke many of the promises of God over our lives for a long time. We have seen, and are still seeing, God bring them to pass in our lives.

Objects and animals in a dream or vision are symbolic. A car in a dream represents ministry. If you are the one driving the car, it is your ministry. God is showing you; however, if you see someone in the back seat of the car they are the ones supporting the ministry. Supporting could be either financially or spiritually. Below is a list of different things which God has revealed to us the meaning of. Sometimes things can have more than one meaning.

These are the interpretations of things God has shown us:

Vision of Heaven

I believe many people have had visions of heaven in different ways. For example, seeing the angels in heaven, the streets of gold, the pearly gates, or the crystal water. Revelation 21:21, "And the twelve gates were twelve pearls: every several gate was of one pearl: and the street of the city was pure gold, as it were transparent glass." I believe because of how it happened in my life, that when God is making the call on your life as a Prophet of God, you will experience seeing the Throne Room of God like no other vision or experience before. When this happened in my life, I clearly saw the heavens being opened up and there I was in the midst of the Throne Room of God. It was so glorious. The angels of the Lord were everywhere. I was there for sometime when all of a sudden a great multitude of gargoyles were coming at me. God was showing me the trials and tribulations that were about to come in my life, to take me up into a higher realm of the spirit. I believe the call on Prophet Isaiah's life was similar. Isaiah 6:1-7, "In the year that king Uzziah died I saw also the Lord sitting upon a throne, high and lifted up, and his train filled the temple. Above it stood the seraphims: each one had six wings; with twain he covered his face, and with twain he covered his feet, and with twain he did fly. And one cried unto another, and said, Holy, holy, holy, is the Lord of hosts: the whole earth is full of his glory. And the posts of the door moved at the voice of him that cried, and the house was filled with smoke. Then said I, Woe is me! For I am undone; because I am a man of unclean lips, and I dwell in the midst of a people of unclean lips: for mine eyes have seen the King, the Lord of hosts. Then flew one of the seraphims unto me, having a live coal in his hand, which he had taken with the tongs from off the altar: and he laid it upon my mouth, and said, Lo, this hath touched thy lips; and thine iniquity is taken away, and thy sin purged."

Vision of Hell

A young man who knew he was called to be a Prophet of God was playing around with his spiritual life and God gave him a vision of himself in hell, in a prison behind bars, and above that prison he saw the word "Prophet" written. The Word of God says that the gifts and calling of God are irrevocable and without repentance. We need to look at the parable in Luke 16:19-31, the story about the rich man and Lazarus. The rich man, when he was alive, never did anything for the kingdom of God. When he was in hell, he wanted to fulfill his Evangelistic call; he wanted someone to be sent to his brothers to hear the gospel. (Verses 27, 28.)

When ministering to a Pastor and his wife, God showed me a vision of hell and in the vision I saw a man. The Lord told me this was the Pastor's brother. When I told the Pastor the vision, he explained to me that his brother was also a Pastor and that he had not spoken to him for years because of an ought his brother had against him. The Lord was revealing this, so that the Pastor we were ministering to could go to his brother and humble himself so that his brother's salvation would not be at risk.

Once, while in a congregation, the people were in the spirit and we asked God to first give them a revelation of heaven. After that we asked God to give them all a revelation of Hell. When they saw the revelation of Hell, one woman began screaming and couldn't come out, until praying for her, so the anointing was lifted. The Lord showed me that

105

because this woman was in fornication, her spirit didn't want to come out. This happened at another church when we were in Honduras. The congregation had a revelation of hell and they all began to scream violently. The police came in to see what was going on. The whole church needed deliverance. It wasn't until we prayed that their spirits were able to come out of the revelation of hell.

Hell is real! Jesus spoke more about Hell than He did heaven because He desires that none should go there. Hell was made for satan and his demons, not for man. The Word of God shows that because of the lack of knowledge, many of God's people are in captivity. Because we are not doing what God called us to do, many are going to Hell and Hell is expanding everyday. Isaiah 5:13, 14, "Therefore my people are gone into captivity, because they have no knowledge: and their honourable men are famished, and their multitude dried up with thirst. Therefore Hell hath enlarged herself, and opened her mouth without measure: and their glory, and their multitude, and their pomp, and he that rejoiceth, shall descend into it."

Car — Represents a ministry for the person driving and in the front seat of the car.
If you see people in the backseat of the car, they would be the ones supporting the ministry. God showed me in a dream a beautiful Excalibur car, which represented the ministry He has given us.

Bicycle — Local Evangelistic ministry for the church.

Motorcycle — Same as bicycle, just covering a larger area.

Helicopter — Represents a Local Ministry, such as ministering to the homeless, the prisons, nursing homes, etc.

Airplane — Represents or symbolic of an International Ministry.

Visions of the Armour of God – Divine Equipment for Warfare.
(Ephesians 6:10-18)

Helmet	Salvation
Breast Plate	Righteousness
Girded Loins	Truth
Shield	Faith
Sword	Word of God
Feet Shod	The Gospel of Peace

Once while in Mexico, the Lord showed me in a vision a lot of little children with helmets on. That day, as we were driving, we stopped by a roadside stand where they were selling food and refreshments. About 20 young children all gave their hearts to Jesus. (Salvation) Ephesians 6:17, "And take the helmet of salvation, and the sword of the Spirit, which is the Word of God."

A man of God was struggling with problems in his life and saw himself in a vision, in the midst of a battle, without a helmet or shoes on. The Lord revealed his salvation was at stake and he had no right preaching the gospel if he wasn't living it. (Psalm 50:16, 17), "But unto the wicked God saith, "What hast thou to do to declare my statutes, or that thou shouldest take my covenant in thy mouth? Seeing thou hatest instruction and castest my words behind thee.""

Several ways you may see the Sword of God in Visions:

The Sword in a sheath – God was showing me that person did not know how to use the Word of God.

The Sword sharp only on one side - Someone not fully walking in Spirit and Truth.

The Double Edge Sword sharp on both sides and held up — Ready for Battle. Full of the Word of God. John 3:34, "For he who God hath sent speaketh the words of God: for God giveth not the Spirit by measure unto him. You may also see this sword very shiny.

The Hand and Fingers Representative of the Five Fold Ministry

Left Hand — Calling, but not yet developed or trained up in their Office or Calling.

Right Hand — Ordained before God and Man into their Office or Calling.

Thumb — Apostle; the thumb can touch all the other fingers. Needs to know each office and watch over the other four offices or callings. A Spiritual Father.

Index Finger — Prophet; pointer finger, a Prophet likes to point out what is going on in the hearts of God's people.

Middle Finger — Evangelists; the longest finger, has the greatest outreach because their concern is for souls.

Ring Finger — Pastor; the Pastors are married to the church, looking out for its' needs.

Pinky Finger — Teacher; the smallest finger. The Teachers breakdown and simplify the Word of God so we can easily apply it to our lives.

★★ The Finger of God represents the Holy Spirit. Luke 11:20, "But if I with the Finger of God cast out devils, no doubt the Kingdom of God is come upon you. Matthew 12:28 says, "But I cast out devils by the Spirit of God,…."

Deuteronomy 9:10, "And the Lord delivered unto me two tables of stone written with the finger of God.

Visions of Colors — God also uses colors to communicate with us.

Amber	Red and yellow mixed and bright. I heard it was the Fire and compassion of the Lord mixed which brings forth Revelation. The Glory of God. Ezekiel 1:4, 8:2
Black	A lot of times when we see black we think it is evil, death and sin; as according to Lamentations 4:6-8, Lamentations 3:6.
	God also inhabits darkness as the Word says in Psalms 18:9 & 11, He made darkness His secret place.
	Exodus 20:21; Moses drew near unto the thick darkness where God was.
Blue	Presence of God - Exodus 28:37, "Blue Lace". Holiness to the Lord! Water – River of God – Representing Word of God.

Gold   Love of God. Malachi 3:3, "And he shall sit as a refiner and purifier of silver: and he shall purify the sons of Levi, and purge them as gold and silver, that they may offer unto the Lord an offering in righteousness." When gold is put into the fire it is refined; just as we are when we go through the furnace of affliction and we come out the other side, having the love and mercy of God for others. Isaiah 48:10, "Behold, I have refined thee, but not with silver, I have chosen thee in the furnace of affliction."

Revelation 3:18 – "Gold tried by Fire."

Green   Represents the Peace of God; Psalms 23:2, "He maketh me to lie down in green pastures." Being in the throne room of God - (Emeralds) In a vision I saw a beautiful large riverbed of emeralds, (brilliantly sparkling, a very rich green color) with a Glistening White light in the background – Revelation 4:3, A rainbow round about the throne, in sight like unto an emerald. In a vision, God showed me the spiritual giftings He had for me as I continued to seek Him. Green also represents money, riches and wealth. Psalm 112:1-3, "Praise ye the Lord. Blessed is the man that feareth the Lord,...." And verse 3, "Wealth and Riches shall be in his house."

Multi-color   Favor of God and man. Example: Joseph's father made him a robe of many colors. Genesis 37:3, "Now Israel loved Joseph more than all his children, because he was the son of his old age; and he made him a coat of many colors.

Can also stand for a Covenant made such as the covenant God made with Noah symbolized by the rainbow. Genesis 9:14, 15, "And it shall come to pass, when I bring a cloud over the earth, that the bow shall be seen in the cloud: and I will remember my covenant, which is between me and you and every living creature of all flesh; and the waters shall no more become a flood to destroy all flesh."

Orange | New Beginnings, New Horizons. Sunrises. Proven by Fire.

Pink | Compassion, New Heart, Ezekiel 36:26, "A new heart also will I give you, and a new spirit will I put within you and I will take away the stony heart out of your flesh and I will give you a heart of flesh."

Purple | Royalty, Kingsly anointing, majestic sonship, and a sign of Wealth. II Chronicles 2:7, Esther 1:6, Luke 16:19

Red | Blood, Atonement (Scarlet) Isaiah 1:18. Like the Blood of Jesus covering our sins. Red Robe – represents the Kingsly Anointing, Apostolic.

Red – blood can also represent a spirit of violence, blood shed in that place.

Silver | Prosperity - Job 22:25, "Yea the Alimighty shall be thy defence, and thou shalt have plenty of silver. Wisdom, refining, purification. Zechariah 13:9, "And I will bring the third part through the fire and will refine them as silver is refined, and I will try them as Gold is tried...."

White | Purity, Light, Wisdom, Holiness Daniel 12:10, Mark 9:13, Revelation 7:9, 7:14, Revelation 1:14. White Raiment - Holiness. Revelation 3:18. Army of the Lord – Bride of Christ. Revelation 19:14.

Yellow | Joy, Revelation. Depending on the vision or dream, yellow (If it is a dingy yellow) can mean something old.

Animals, Objects, and Other Symbols

Alligators — Represents Trouble; Usually from someone who is close to you.

Almonds — Almond or Almond Tree is representative of fruitfulness. Numbers 17:8.

Baptism — Represents new man. In one vision there was an angel changing the person's garments. Zechariah 3:3, 4, "Now Joshua was clothed with filthy garments, and stood before the angel. And he answered and spake unto those that stood before him, saying, Take away the filthy garments from him. And unto him he said, Behold, I have caused thine iniquity to pass from thee, and I will clothe thee with change of raiment."

Balances — When shown level this is a person with integrity. Job 31:6, "Let me be weighed in an even balance, that God may know mine integrity."

Bears — Represent Fear.

Bees — Attack of the enemy to sting or hurt.

Psalm 118:12, "They compassed me about like bees; they are quenched as the fire of thorns: for in the name of the Lord I will destroy them."

Boat — Established on the Word of God. (Deep blue water is the true revelations of God's Word.)

Cats — Usually represents Lust.

Cedar Tree — Building up of God's House – While driving to the state of Georgia, I had a vision of very tall cedar trees. I heard the Lord say these are the Cedars of Lebanon. God wanted to build His church there. I Kings 5:5, "...and behold, I purpose to build an house unto the name of the Lord my God..." Verse

6, "Now therefore command thou that they hew me cedar trees out of Lebanon…"

In another vision, when we were going to Central America to minister, I saw very tall black, barren cedar trees– which represented the lack of prosperity and fruitfulness of the things of God.

City

I had a vision of a whole city that was turned upside down. God was showing what He was about to do there: Deliverance, Healing, etc. Isaiah 24:1, "Behold, the Lord maketh the earth empty, and maketh it waste, and turneth it upside down,…" Psalms 146:9, "…the wicked he turneth upside down."

Another time when we were ministering, I had an inner vision of Chicago Meigs Airport and a Beech 18 airplane. When I spoke it out, it meant something to the person we were ministering to. Her kids who lived in Chicago were coming to visit her. She said, "Oh, that can't be because my kids are driving here to see me." The next day she received a call from her daughter saying they had purchased discounted tickets and would be flying in from Chicago to see her.

Cows

Prosperity because of the meat and the milk.

Crutch

In a vision, a person was walking with a crutch – The Lord revealed that they were not one with their spouse and their walk was being affected.

Dogs

You need to first recognize what kind of a dog it is because certain dogs are known to have certain demeanors. For instance, a Doberman pinscher or a rottweiler are considered to be more ferocious than a poodle. So, by knowing the characteristics of any animal, it should give you more understanding of what the vision or dream means. Example: One time in our home, there was another man of God staying with us. The Lord showed in a vision him looking like a Dalmatian (remember this breed is white with black or brown spots). God was showing us that this represented a false humility.

Philippians 3:2 says, "Beware of dogs, beware of evil workers, beware of the concision. Many times dogs represent unclean spirits or something of the enemy.

Door	Open door represents God opening doors, making the way for you. Unlimited opportunities. I Corinthians 16:9, "For a great door and effectual is opened unto me and there are many adversaries."
	Heavenly Door – God showing you have access to enter into the heavens for the Father to give you the revelations. John 1:51, "….Hereafter ye shall see heaven open,…"
Doves	Little white doves – On our way to minister in a church, I had a vision of many little white doves flying in the Church. The Lord was showing me he had a prophetic word for many of the people in the church. It reminded me of how God used the dove to let Noah know if the waters were abated from off the earth. (Genesis 8:11)
Eagle	Prophetic call – if it is a small eagle – person is still being trained up.
Eagle Owl	Prophetic Discerning and Deliverance Anointing. While praying for my husband once God showed me a vision of an Owl with Eagle Wings. There is a bird called the Eurasian Eagle Owl – they are night creatures, and they eat just about anything moving, whether in the air or on the ground. God was showing the Powerful Prophetic Discerning and Deliverance Anointing He had given my husband.

Eyes	Eyes as a Flaming Fire, are the Eyes of God. Rev. 1:14, "His head and his hairs were white like wool, as white as snow; and his eyes were as a flame of fire;"—showing the penetrating insight God has to everything.
	I have seen mean, evil, glaring eyes looking at me. The enemy was mad because the place we were ministering at had been his territory for so long. (Many people in that place were in fornication, adultery, etc.) When the Lord revealed this and God began to expose this for His people to come to repentance, I saw the glaring angry eyes of the enemy because he was losing his grip on those people.
	Rays coming from the eyes – Spirit of Wisdom.
Feet	Beautiful Feet – Preaching Good News. Romans 10:15, "How beautiful are the feet of them that preach the Gospel of Peace and bring glad tidings of good things."
	Feet on Someone's neck – Victory over the enemy.
	Joshua 10:24-26; God gave Joshua the victory over the 5 kings and he instructed the captains of his army to put their feet on the kings' necks. And then Joshua proclaimed: so shall the Lord do to all your enemies that fight against you.
Fingers Touching	Vision such as the picture where fingers are together touching – refers to discernment using the senses. Hebrews 5:13, 14, "For everyone that useth milk is unskillful in the word of righteousness for he is a babe, but strong meat belongeth to them that are of full age, even those who by reason of use have their senses exercised to discern both good and evil."

Fish	Souls coming into the kingdom of God.

I saw in a vision, two multi-colored orange wide mouthed fish. The fish's mouth were open and making a grunting sound. I asked what the vision meant and the Lord revealed the person was involved in orgies.

Fishhooks	God taking away posterity (even in the spiritual). Amos 4:2, "The Lord God hath sworn by his holiness, that, lo, the days shall come upon you, that he will take you away with hooks, and your posterity with fishhooks." Not heeding to the Word of the Lord.

Fishhooks with bait on them – Represents winning souls for the Lord. Like Jesus told Peter He was going to make him a Fisher of Men. (Matthew 4:19)

Frogs	Unclean spirits. Revelation 16:13, "And I saw three unclean spirits like frogs come out of the mouth of the dragon…." We were praying deliverance over a man of God once, and as we began to pray, out of his mouth came a sound like the sound a frog makes.
Gnat	Backbiting and gossiping. We went to minister in a place that had swarms of gnats — it was because there was so much backbiting going on there. Galatians 5:15, "But if ye bite and devour one another, take heed that ye be not consumed one of another."
Gorilla Face	While in Suriname, South America, we ministered in many churches; one night after ministering deliverance to a whole congregation, in the middle of the night I awoke to see what looked like a stickman with a gorilla face. When I shared it with the Pastor, he said this was the false god the "Bush Negroes" use to worship over there.

Hair Ball	Spirit of Lust – Sometimes you can even feel like it is stuck in the back of your throat, or like little fuzzies are all around someone when you touch them.
Hammer	The Word of God is like a hammer when someone is in sin and needs correction. (Jeremiah 23:29)
Helmet	Represents Salvation – Ephesians 6:17, "…the helmet of salvation.
Honey	Revelations. When King Saul's son, Jonathan, had tasted the honey, his eyes were enlightened. I Samuel 14:27, "But Jonathan heard not when his father charged the people with the oath; wherefore he put forth the end of the rod that was in his hand, and dipped it in an honeycomb, and put his hand to his mouth; and his eyes were enlightened."
	Honey mixed with milk – the promises of God.
	(The Land of Milk and Honey)
Hornet	God uses the Hornet as a weapon against the enemy coming at us to give us our land. One morning, as I was rising from sleep, I had a vision of a hornet just sitting on our kitchen floor. Exodus 23:28, "And I will send hornets before thee, which shall drive out the Hivite, the Canaanite, and the Hittite from before thee." (Deuteronomy 7:20, Joshua 24:12)
Keys	Authority given in the realm of the spirit. Matthew 16:19, "And I will give unto thee the keys of the kingdom of heaven…."
Kingsly Robe	Representative of Apostolic calling and anointing because of the power and authority God has placed on the Apostolic.
Lamb	The Lord showed me a big lamb turned upside down – the lamb represented a particular church and the leader was getting ready to divorce his wife and

marry another woman. The Lamb was completely helpless. From what I have heard, when a lamb falls on it's back it needs help to get back up.

Leopard   Sneaky, ferocious, and ready to destroy. A woman came to us because of a problem with her leader in the church. I saw a black leopard ready to take her as it's prey. The woman was very intelligent' and had a professional career. However, the Lord revealed the male leader had a perverted spirit and was after her and her beautiful sixteen year old daughter. The woman did not take heed and the enemy used that man to try to destroy them. Daniel 7:6-8 speaks about the beast looking like a leopard ready to devour. From this experience I saw how the perverted spirit out ranks the intellect spirit.

Lightening   Seeing lightening in the realm of the spirit sometimes means God is trying to speak – possibly even through the prophetic tongue. Exodus 20:18, 19; "And all the people saw the thunderings, and lightnings, and the noise of the trumpet, and the mountain smoking: and when the people saw it, they removed, and stood afar off. And they said unto Moses, Speak thou with us, and we will hear but let not God speak with us, lest we die."

Lock Ness

Monster   Spirit of Justification; In the realm of the spirit it has a long neck – looks like the pictures shown of the legendary Lock Ness monster. Job 41:1, "Canst thou draw out leviathan with an hook? Or his tongue with a cord which thou lettest down?"

Mailbox   Letters coming out of mailbox – gift of discernment. I Corinthians 12:10, "....to another discerning of spirits. God revealing the secrets of people's hearts to you. I Corinthians 14:25.

117

	Angels putting letters in mailbox – God has a message for you.
Mantles	Can look like a cape, a robe, or a blanket.

Red Robe — Represents Kingsly Anointing

Cape – Prophet Anointing

Long Three/Quarter Length – Prophetic Overseer (Like Elijah's mantle – II Kings 2:13, 14.)

Blanket – Glory of God; it is very heavy, weighty. (II Chronicles 7:1; when God's Glory was there no one could even move to preach.)

Masks	Mime Face – Controlled by something, counterfeit, fake.

Bear wearing mask – appearing to be something or someone else but hiding behind fear.

Monkeys	I once saw a vision of a woman who appeared to be like a monkey covering it's eyes, ears, etc. The Lord was showing me she did not want to see or hear anything the Lord had to say through our lives. Spirit of Rebellion. Ezekiel 12:2, "Son of man thou dwellest in the midst of a rebellious house; which have eyes to see, and see not; they have ears to hear, and hear not: for they are a rebellious house."
Naked	Without a covering; John ran when his covering, Jesus, had been taken from him. Mark 14:52. Same for the sons of Sceva in Acts 19:13, they were naked (the demons or evil spirits had stripped them from their clothes); I believe it was because they were hopping from church to church and had no covering. That is why they called them vagabonds in verse 13.

Shame – Isaiah 20:2-4; verse 4, "...naked and barefoot, even with their buttocks uncovered, to the shame of Eygpt." Revelation 16:15, "Behold, I come as a thief. Blessed is he that watcheth, and keepeth his garments, lest he walk naked, and they see his shame."

In Sin – Rebellion toward God; like King Saul in I Samuel 19:23, 24, when he came in the presence of the anointing he stripped off his clothes... and he was exposed. The same was for King Ahaz: Rebellion, II Chronicles 28:19; "For the Lord brought Judah low because of Ahaz king of Israel; for he made Judah naked, and transgressed sore against the Lord."

Net	Fish net can represent catching fish – souls.
	A Flattering tongue will also put a net out there for the enemy to catch his prey. Proverbs 29:5, "A man that flattereth his neighbour spreadeth a net for his feet."
Oval Mirror	God showed a vision of an oval mirror while interceding for an Apostle of God......the Lord was revealing that the Man of God was moving in the highest realm of the spirit with the wisdom of God.
Owl	Night Creature — able to see and discern the demonic forces affecting people.
Palm Tree	Prosper, succeed, to thrive, Psalm 92:12, "The righteous shall flourish like the palm tree: he shall grow like a cedar in Lebanon." Flourish.
Panther	While ministering to a woman, I saw a black panther ready to leap on her. This animal is considered very fierce. God was trying to warn her about being

involved with a man that the Lord had revealed had a very controlling, manipulating jezebel spirit.

Photos   Pictures or Albums represent holding on to the past.

Rainbow   God showing that His covenant is established in your life and He will bring His promises to pass for you.

River   River of Clear Pure Water is the Holy Spirit. John 7:38, "He that believeth on me, as the scripture hath said, out of his belly shall flow rivers of living water."

Rod or Scepter   Represents authority – Aarons rod. Numbers 17:3-8. Esther – Favor of God.

Roman Numerals   This is symbolizing they are living by the law, not the grace.

Scroll   God wanting you to eat the Word of God – apply the Word to your life. (Ezekiel 3:1-3)

Seal of God   It almost looks like a stamp or a shield such as a family crest. Ephesians 4:30, "And grieve not the Holy Spirit of God, whereby ye are sealed unto the day of redemption."

Snakes   Depending on the type of snake. If it is a bunch of little black snakes; it usually represents gossip.

Vipers – venomous snake – Religious Spirit, trying to poison persons mind with religious beliefs. Matthew 3:7, "But when he saw many of the Pharisees and Sadducees come to his baptism, said unto them, O generation of vipers, who hath warned you to flee from the wrath to come?" Also, the venom could be from listening to gossip because the Word of God is very clear that if we gossip or listen to gossip we are defiled and have fallen from the grace of God.

Hebrews 12:14, 15, "Follow peace with all men, and holiness, without which no man shall see the Lord: Looking diligently lest any man fail of the grace of God; lest any root of bitterness springing up trouble you and thereby many be defiled."

A boa constrictor tries to squeeze the life out of you; that life is Jesus.

A python usually represents someone having been involved in the psychic or witchcraft. An example is the woman in Acts 16:16, she had a spirit of divination.

A large snake you see in the realm of the spirit in someone can be from a sexual violation. (Can represent violation or incest.)

When you dream of a snake with his tongue out, that is God showing you that deliverance is about to take place in your life. The senses of a snake are in the tongue and the Lord is showing you that the enemy knows he is about to be evicted.

Spiders	Represents confusion. Confusion comes when we cannot hear from God. Our voice brings confusion. In Ezra 9:5-7; when the heavens were closed because of iniquity; Verse 7, "….and to confusion of face, as it is this day."
Spider webs	A trap of the enemy.
Swine – Pig	Someone keeps doing the same thing against God. II Peter 2:22, "But it is happened unto them according to the true proverb, the dog is turned to his own vomit again; and the sow that was washed to her wallowing in the mire."
Toilet	Represents deliverance.

Tree	Olive Tree – Prosperous and full of God's mercy. Psalm 52:8, "But I am like a green olive tree in the House of God, I trust in the mercy of God forever and ever."
Trumpet	The Voice of the Prophetic Utterance: Isaiah 58:1, "Cry aloud, spare not, lift up thy voice like a trumpet, and shew my people their transgression, and the house of Jacob their sins." Symbolic of the Prophetic Call – Prophet Declaring The Word of the Lord.
	Prophetic Utterance to lead the people – Numbers 10:1-10.
Vultures	Unclean Spirits – Leviticus 11:13, 14.
	Fault Finding – like eating road kill. Job 28:7, "There is a path which no fowl knoweth, and which the vulture's eye hath not seen:" – In other words, who are we if God has forgiven; how can we still hold it against them.
Waterfall	Word of God richly in person's life. When seeing a waterfall like Niagara Falls — showing generating power.
Wolverine	Having been involved in Martial Arts. While ministering a young man began to manifest; he looked like a wolverine and began to crawl up walls trying to get away. When the demonic spirit spoke, it said it was the one who started martial arts.
Woman with Many arms	A false god that the Hindu people worship. A woman we ministered to, while manifesting, the demon spoke out and said they were kali.

Visions and Dreams and the Interpretation Received

Many times we will see things that make no sense to us, but they do to the person we are ministering to. An example of this is, one time when we were ministering to a young lady, I had an inner vision of a sewing machine. When I spoke it out the young lady immediately began to cry because her grandmother, who had always taken care of her and raised her from a very early age, use to sew her clothes for her and had died while still caring for her. Because of this, the young lady had held on to anger and unforgiveness toward God for many years. When we ministered to her, she released the unforgiveness and anger and was delivered and made free by the Power of God. Glory to the Lord!

Written below are more visions and dreams God gave and the understanding received for them. By hearing these dreams and visions and the understanding God has given, hopefully, they will help you to understand the visions and dreams God is giving you. Build the relationship with the Holy Spirit. He dwells in you if you are a born again believer. (John 3:3, Acts 1:4, 5)

About 13 years ago, my husband and I went to Pensacola, Florida to a place called Brownsville. There were many, many people coming from all over the world because they had heard there was a mighty rival going on there. The spirit of repentance was very heavy there and the Evangelist and Pastor in that church always preached on repentance. In the Sunday morning worship service, the place was filled with people praising and worshiping the Lord Jesus. All of the sudden, I heard the roar of waves which sounded like the ocean was in that place. Revelation 1:15 speaks of God's voice in this way; "And his feet like unto fine brass, as if they burned in a furnace and his voice of the sound of many waters." Also, in Ezekiel 43:2 it describes God's voice; "And behold, the glory of the God of Israel came from the way of the east: and his voice was like a noise of many waters: and the earth shined with His glory." At the same time, I saw above us in the sanctuary what looked like a bluish grey cloud. Not knowing what it was, I blinked my eyes to try to clear them and when I opened my eyes I saw angels hovering wingtip to wingtip filling the whole place. It was a tremendous sight and my spirit leaped and rejoiced! The Lord revealed to me that because people were truly repenting and getting their hearts right and coming clean with God that His mercy seat was there. If you remember in the Old and New Testament it shows how the cherubims hover over the mercy seat of God. Exodus 25:18-22, also I Kings 6:27, "And he set the cherubims within the inner house: and they stretched forth the wings of the cherubims, so that the wing of the one touched the one wall, and wing of the other cherub touched the other wall; and their wings touched one another in the midst of the house." And also in Hebrews 9:5, "And over it the cherubims of glory shadowing the mercy seat; of which we cannot now speak particularly." What an Awesome God we serve! Who can fathom the mercy of Our Loving and Holy Father.

Once, while praying at the altar in a church located in Daytona Beach, Florida, before the worship service began; I saw in a vision a very old wrinkled up, decrepit lady, who was hunched over and curled up in a ball, almost in a fetal position. Her hair was brown and scraggly and the skin on her face was very dark and wrinkled like leather, as if she had been in the sun for many, many years. I continued praying and asking the Lord what or who this was. I heard very clearly, "This is my bride." My spirit became very sorrowful because the Word of God says in Ephesians 5:27, "That he might present it to himself a glorious church, not having spot, or wrinkle, or any such thing, but that it should be holy and without blemish." It was at this point that God began revealing to me how desperately the Body of Christ needs deliverance. Many people proclaiming Jesus Christ as their Lord and Saviour; and they're still in fornication, adultery, addictions, and are full of unforgiveness, bitterness, and resentment. We need to be separated mind, will, and emotions like the Word of God says in I Thessalonians 5:23, "And the very God of peace sanctify you wholly; and I pray God your whole spirit and soul and body be preserved blameless unto the coming of our Lord Jesus Christ." Throughout the Word of God, God's people needed deliverance; same for us. Through this, God showed me the importance of getting the anointing, walking in the anointing, and living in that anointing that God's people would be delivered and healed everywhere we went.

While praying one morning, I saw the brilliancy of a bright white light. Then I saw transparent, like blue translucent, veils all around me and as I entered in, I sensed the presence of the Lord. In front of me, I saw a large package wrapped. The wrapping paper was plaid; however, it had a beautiful clear transparent wrapping over it and a bow on the outside. What I felt the Lord was showing me was that as I was in His Holy presence, He had a spiritual gift for me and the reason for the plaid wrapping was it would be for everyday use; and the beauty of the gift was illustrated by the translucent outward wrapping and bow on it.

A woman saw herself where her spirit was out of her body and she was looking down at herself as she was asleep. God was trying to show her that her life was passing her by as she had not totally stepped into her call. Hebrews 6:12; "That ye be not slothful, but followers of them who through faith and patience inherit the promises."

Another vision was where there were two eyes staggered; one up and one down and between them you could see the sun and the moon. The sun was above and the moon lower. When asking God for the understanding, this is what was received: God had established the promises He had made to us in the Heavens and in the Earth and He was watching over us that all would come to pass.

PROPHECY

Prophecy!! What is Prophecy? Prophecy is the foretelling of what is to come that was divinely revealed or inspired by God to us. In accordance to the Word of God in Revelation 19:10, "…for the testimony of Jesus is the spirit of prophecy." God desires that relationship with us that He can reveal and fulfill the prophecies that have been spoken. Prophecy is not witchcraft and moving in the prophetic is not witchcraft. However, when we put a price tag on it, we've allowed ourselves to step over the boundaries of God and we are operating in a spirit of divination and witchcraft. In other words, when someone charges or puts a price on speaking forth what God has to say, then this is from a spirit of divination. Read what the Word of God says in Micah 3:11, "The heads thereof judge for reward, and the priests thereof teach for hire, and the prophets thereof divine for money: yet will they lean upon the Lord, and say, Is not the Lord among us? None evil can come upon us?" In other words, people having conferences about "How to hear from God?" or "How to know the voice of God?" or any conference that you have to pay to get into to learn the things of the Word of God, these are not of the Lord. Love offerings and blessings the people want to give the Man or Woman of God is pleasing unto the Lord, but to charge for the Gospel of Jesus Christ is going against Our Holy God. Some people are so hungry for the things of God and they are looking for the truth and we need to be in accordance to the Word of God in Matthew 10:8, "Heal the sick, cleanse the lepers, raise the dead, cast out devils: freely ye have received, freely give." If someone is trying to charge you, I would suggest you spend your money on a Bible – That is the Voice of God!! Hear what is being said; tithes and offerings you have to bring into the storehouse where you are getting fed; because in accordance with Malachi 3:8-12, this is the only time in the Bible where it says if you don't pay your tithes and offerings you will be cursed with a curse and God cannot rebuke the devourer in your life. Remember a laborer is worthy of his hire. (Luke 10:7) When Jesus said, "I must be about my Father's business;" He didn't mean sell the Gospel. Today, many of us have made the Gospel of Jesus Christ a business and the Lord wants this to stop. I Peter 4:17, "For the time is come that judgment must begin at the house of God: and if it first begin at us, what shall the end be of them that obey not the gospel of God?" When God sends us out, He supplies. This reminds me of a sign I saw in a convenient store; the sign which was next to a little bowl of pennies said, "Got a Penny, Give a Penny; Need a Penny, Take a Penny; Need Two Pennies, Get a JOB!" God will make a way and provide for you when it is His timing. Not only will God provide when He sends you on a mission but when you return He always has a blessing waiting for you. An example is Abraham in Genesis 14:16-20 when Abraham went to go rescue and deliver Lot and his family. When Abraham brought them out of captivity God met Abraham thru Melchizedek, king of Salem (which represents Jesus), and He brought him bread and wine, refreshing Abraham in Spirit and Truth. The Word of God says in I Corinthians 14:1, "Follow after charity, and desire spiritual gifts, but rather that ye may prophesy. So, we should desire this with a passion; Apostle Paul said it this way: "Wherefore, brethren, covet to prophecy, and forbid not to speak with tongues." Prophets Prophesy, Prophets Prophesy, Prophets Prophesy: Declare the Word of the Lord and let your voices be heard for the Glory of the Lord.Prophecy is for comfort, edification, and exhortation as written in I Corinthians 14:3. The Gift of Prophecy is given by the Holy Spirit as it is written in I Corinthians 12:10. As mentioned before, we need to desire to prophesy; I believe the reason we should strongly desire this is that we can be there for others to encourage them and lift them up in their walk with the Lord! When you desire the Gift of Prophecy, you are also declaring that you want to be separated for the Lord to hear His Voice. An example in the Old Testament of someone who was separated for God to declare His Word that he might prophesy is Enoch. Enoch was and is a true Prophet of God. The Word of God declares that he was so separated for the Lord that he could declare that his life was pleasing unto God. Hebrews 11:5, "By faith Enoch was translated that he should not see death; and was not found, because God had translated him; for before his translation he had this testimony, that he pleased God." Prophet Enoch's life was so pleasing that God translated him as well as Prophet Elijah for the last days so that the Prophetic Word — The Prophecy that Jesus is the Messiah they awaited for can be brought forth and revealed unto the Jewish people in the time of tribulation. Read Revelation 11:3-6, "And I will give power unto my two witnesses, and they shall prophesy a thousand two hundred and threescore days, clothed in sackcloth. These are the two olive trees, and the two candlesticks standing before the God of the earth. And if any man will hurt them, fire proceedeth out of their mouth, and devoureth their enemies: and if any man will hurt them, he must in this manner be killed. These have power to shut heaven that it rain not in the days of their prophecy: and have power over waters to turn them to blood, and to smite the earth with all plagues, as often as they will." Now that is moving in Prophecy with power. They will be prophesying for 3 and ½ years! Tremendous! Glory to God!

In the Old Testament, there is an example in II Samuel 16:23 when Ahithophel gave prophetic counsel it says, "And the counsel of Ahithophel, which he counseled in those days, was as if a man had inquired at the Oracle of God: ...." That means in the presence of God, the Holy of Holies to hear God's wisdom and counsel." (The Oracle of God is described in I Kings 6:5, 6:16, 6:19-23, 6:31 and in I Peter 4:11 which says, "If any man speak, let him speak the oracles of God; ...") Prophecy is also spoken of as the Oracles of God; bringing forth the wisdom from the throne of God as we have received it from Our Father. In seeking the Lord, I was crying out to Him for more; more of Him, and to be used mightily for His Kingdom. I was glorifying, honoring, and thanking God for how He was and is using me in revealing things unto me, especially the secrets of people's hearts; (I Corinthians 14:25), revealing the past and the present so that they can be delivered, made free, and going forward in the Lord. In Prophecy, the past allows us to go into people's hearts revealing how and when the spirits entered them so that we can minister deliverance to them and they can be free. In Prophecy, the present allows us to see what they are doing now and to know the gifts and callings in their lives and how God wants to use them. In Prophecy, the future not only allows you to see for the individual what God has, but also that you can see corporately which effects many, many more people. Inside of me my spirit yearns and groans for more of Him and while in His presence, I was asking the Lord for more in the area of Prophecy for the future – seeing even more and more into the future. Let me tell you, God never ceases to amaze me: He always answers and He answers exceedingly abundantly above all that we could ever ask or think. (Ephesians 3:20) In my search and hunger for this, God placed it in my spirit to read the book of Prophet Daniel again. God was showing me by looking at the life of Prophet Daniel what the key is to moving mightily in future prophecy.

Let us go together through the book of Daniel. As I began looking at Prophet Daniel's life in chapter 1; I noticed Daniel was just a child of 13 or 14 years old when he was taken captive and they made him a eunuch for King Nebuchadnezzar. You understand; they cut off his testicles (his balls): they castrated him. Daniel could have had bitterness, resentment, and unforgiveness, but instead Daniel never complained. Basically, he said, even though I am in captivity and even though they have castrated me, I choose to go even more out for my God by not defiling myself with the food and drink of the king. Prophet Daniel chose to put his flesh in submission to his spirit and eat that which was healthier for him. Daniel 1:8, "But Daniel purposed in his heart that he would not defile himself with the portion of the king's meat, nor with the wine which he drank: therefore he requested of the prince of the eunuchs that he might not defile himself." I believe because of this God blessed Daniel with understanding in all visions and dreams. (Daniel 1:17, "As for these four children, God gave them knowledge and skill in all learning and wisdom: and Daniel had understanding in all visions and dreams.")

Then in Daniel chapter 2, King Nebuchadnezzar dreamed a dream of which troubled his spirit when he awoke. However, he couldn't even remember the dream. So, the king called all the magicians, astrologers, sorcerers, and all kinds of witchcraft to give him the dream and the understanding; of course, they couldn't. They said if you tell us the dream, we can tell you what it means. In other words, they could make up something or fake it. When they couldn't help the King, he became very furious and said, "Let all the wise men of Babylon be killed." (This would have included Prophet Daniel and the three Hebrew boys as well.) When Prophet Daniel heard this, he desired to see the King to speak to him. Daniel knew His God and knew that His God was more than able; and because Daniel had favor with God and King Nebuchadnezzar, he went in to speak to the King. Prophet Daniel said to King Nebuchadnezzar, "Give me time and I know, not only will My God reveal the dream unto me, but He will also give the understanding of the dream." Prophet Daniel immediately went to the three other Hebrew boys in whom he knew he could trust to go into prayer and intercede in this matter. As the three Hebrew boys interceded, the heavens were opened and God Almighty, in a night vision, revealed the dream and the interpretation to Prophet Daniel. Look at how Prophet Daniel glorifies and magnifies the bigness of God. Daniel 2:19-23, "Then was the secret revealed unto Daniel in a night vision. Then Daniel blessed the God of heaven. Daniel answered and said, "Blessed be the name of God for ever and ever for wisdom and might are His. And he changeth the times and the seasons: he removeth kings, and setteth up kings: he giveth wisdom unto the wise, and knowledge to them that know understanding: He revealeth the deep and secret things: he knoweth what is in the darkness, and the light dwelleth with him. I thank thee, and praise thee, O thou God of my fathers, who hast given me wisdom and might, and hast made known unto me now what we desire of thee: for thou hast now made known unto us the king's matter." In all this, King Nebuchadnezzar blessed Daniel mightily with riches and gifts and wanted to make him ruler over the whole province of Babylon and chief of the governors over all the wise men. Prophet Daniel was not interested in position or power. In fact, he said, this is all great, but may I put the other three Hebrew boys in this position because I want to be the Prophet God called me to be, to sit in the gates and be a watchman for God's people. Prophet Daniel's concern was to be the Watchman, the Prophet, God had called him to be. I believe Daniel just wanted to sit in the gate and make sure that the enemy could not come in to destroy. Daniel 2:48, 49, "Then the king made Daniel a great man, and gave him many great gifts, and made him ruler over the whole province of Babylon, and chief of the governors over all the wise men of Babylon. Then Daniel requested of the king, and he set Shadrach, Meshach, and Abednego, over the affairs of the province of Babylon while Prophet Daniel sat in the gate of the king."

In Daniel chapter 3, the three Hebrew boys, who had a close relationship to Prophet Daniel, were put into the fiery furnace because they refused to go against Jehovah God. What we can see from this is that we all have to go through our own trials and tribulations to enter into the kingdom of God. (Acts 14:22 "....and that we must through much tribulation enter into the kingdom of God.") Then in Daniel chapter 4, King Nebuchadnezzar had another dream. Again, the magicians, astrologers, soothsayers, etc. were called in to interpret the dream, but they could not. Then in came Prophet Daniel, a true Prophet of God. By this time years had passed and Daniel had been under King Nebuchadnezzar for sometime. Daniel could have allowed that relationship or that people pleasing spirit to affect him, but he didn't. The dream was a hard word to give and it says in Daniel 4:19 that Daniel was astonied for one hour; that means he pondered on what God had shown him and the interpretation so that he might present it to King Nebuchadnezzar prudently. Prophet Daniel loved the King and when he presented the interpretation to the King he also implored the King to receive his counsel to escape what would come, should the King not receive the warning from the Lord. Daniel 4:27, "Wherefore, O king, let my counsel be acceptable unto thee, and brake off thy sins by righteousness, and thine iniquities by shewing mercy to the poor; if it may be a lengthening of thy tranquillity." Wherefore Prophet Daniel didn't allow friendship, fear of man (the King) or anything to stand in his way of speaking the truth of what God had revealed. God continued to bless Prophet Daniel with the gift of discernment and the gift of interpretation of tongues. (I Corinthians 12:10)

Then in Daniel chapter 5, Belshazzar, King Nebuchadnezzar's son, had a big party and he used the golden and silver vessels that had been taken from the temple in Jerusalem to eat and drink from. In this, the anger of the God was kindled and the writing on the wall came. The psychics, the soothsayers, astrologers, etc. were called to interpret the writing on the wall but they could not interpret what God was trying to say. You see, the enemy cannot understand or interpret tongues, that pure language of God because as it says in I Corinthians 14:2, "For he that speaketh in an unknown tongue speaketh not unto men, but unto God: for no man understandeth him; howbeit in the spirit he speaketh mysteries." Belshazzar was greatly troubled and distraught not knowing what the writing on the wall meant. Then Belshazzar's wife, the queen, reminded him of Prophet Daniel and how God had used him to give King Nebuchadnezzar the interpretations of his dreams, wisdom and understanding, and Godly counsel. (When Belshazzar was doing wrong against God, he didn't have Daniel around him or even know him. That is the same way it is when people don't want to go all out for the Lord, they don't want to be around someone who is.) Prophet Daniel comes in and King Belshazzar said, I will clothe you with scarlet, give you gold, and make you the third ruler in the kingdom. In other words, I will make you famous, give you riches, and give you power and authority if you can interpret the writing on the wall. Daniel again was not interested in the riches, power, or fame. He was a true Prophet of God. His heart was completely for Jehovah God, Jesus Christ. Daniel said you can keep your gifts and give your rewards to someone else because I am here to tell you what God says. Daniel didn't compromise because it was the king. He spoke straight forward to King Belshazzar, saying you saw what happened to your father and yet, instead of humbling yourself and giving God all the glory, you chose to blatantly go against my Holy God. The kingdom of God is all about repentance. As Prophet Daniel spoke and gave the interpretation of the writing, letting King Belshazzar know it is written and established, the kingdom is going to be taken from you. The king should have fallen on his face in repentance to God but instead he still did not humble himself and repent. However, Daniel stood as a Prophet calling people to repentance. That night King Belshazzar was killed.

Then in Daniel chapter 6, Darius the Median began to rule over Babylon and God put Prophet Daniel in favor with the king because the king had observed the spirit of excellence in him. For God to take us to an even higher level in the realm of the spirit, He allows trials and tribulations to come to take us higher. It usually comes from someone close to us. Those that were close to Daniel began to be jealous because of all the favor he had with God and the king and they looked for fault in him. When they couldn't find any fault, they went against the Prophet in his relationship with his God. They tricked King Darius into signing a royal statute stating that if anyone worshipped any God or man beside the king within the next 30 days, they would be thrown into the lions' den. When Daniel heard this decree, he didn't fear man. Daniel feared Jehovah God, Jesus Christ. Luke 12:4, 5 says: "And I say unto you my friends, be not afraid of them that kill the body, and after that have no more that they can do. But I will forewarn you whom ye shall fear: Fear him, which after he hath killed hath power to cast into hell; yea, I say unto you, Fear him." Daniel didn't try to hide when he prayed unto God. In fact, he went in front of the open windows for anyone to see because he was not ashamed of the Gospel of Jesus Christ. Daniel 6:10, "Now when Daniel knew that the writing was signed, he went into his house; and his windows being open in his chamber toward Jerusalem, he kneeled upon his knees three times a day, and prayed, and gave thanks before his God, as he did aforetime." Then those who were coming against Prophet Daniel came to King Darius to gossip about him. They pressured King Darius to uphold the decree he had signed; at which King Darius was very upset and troubled looking for any way he could keep from putting Daniel into the lions' den. However, there was nothing the King could do to change the decree he had signed. But as you know, there is power in the tongue; as the Word of God says in Proverbs 18:21, "Death and Life are in the power of the tongue, and they that love it shall eat the fruit thereof." Darius declared life over Daniel by his words in Daniel 6:16, "...Thy God whom thou servest continually, he will deliver thee." King Darius was so troubled that the Word says he stayed up all night fasting and as soon as it was morning he hurried to the lions den. When King Darius got to the den, he cried out for Daniel. (Daniel 6:20-22, "And when he came to the den he cried with a lamentable voice unto Daniel: and the King spake and said to Daniel, O Daniel, servant of the living God, is thy God, whom thou servest continually able to deliver thee from the lions? Then said Daniel unto the king, O king, live forever. My God hath sent his angel, and hath shut the lions' mouths, that they have not hurt me: forasmuch as before him innocency was found in me: and also before thee, O king, have I done no hurt." Prophet Daniel glorified, magnified, and exalted the King of Kings, Jehovah God; Jesus Christ is His name. Now this is where God really began speaking to me. God showed me that even though many had gone against Prophet Daniel; you might want to say, "Stabbing him in the back," even to the point of having him thrown to the lions, Prophet Daniel did not complain, talk about them, or even want vengeance toward them. In all this, Prophet Daniel showed himself to be a beautiful, awesome, powerful Prophet of God. In this God was so pleased; no wonder, God called Daniel his beloved three times. Now, notice the King, Our King, always has our back as the Word says in Deuteronomy 28:7, "The Lord shall cause thine enemies that rise up against thee to be smitten before thy face: they shall come out against thee one way, and flee before thee seven ways." King Darius didn't play, he cut cancer out right away; he destroyed everything that went against the God of Gods, Jehovah, Our King, and everything that went against the True Prophet of God. He destroyed those men, their wives, and their children. Because Prophet Daniel didn't murmur or complain; because he fully trusted in the Lord, knowing who the true enemy was and is. .... God placed in Prophet Daniel such a heart for souls. Like the Word says, in Proverbs 11:30, "....and he that winneth souls is wise," and in Daniel 12:3, "And they that be wise shall shine as the brightness of the firmament; and they that turn many to righteousness as the stars for ever and ever."

Prophet Daniel's eyes of understanding had been enlightened to understand and see what the Prophet Jeremiah had written that God's people would be in captivity for seventy years. The Prophet then set his face to cry out for God's people for mercy and forgiveness that they might be delivered. Daniel 9:2-5, "In the first year of his reign I, Daniel understood by books the number of the years, whereof the word of the Lord came to Jeremiah the prophet, that he would accomplish seventy years in the desolations of Jerusalem. And I set my face unto the Lord God, to seek by prayer and supplications, with fasting, and sackcloth, and ashes: and I prayed unto the Lord my God, and made my confession, and said, O Lord, the great and dreadful God, keeping the covenant and mercy to them that love him, and to them that keep his commandments; We have sinned, and have committed iniquity, and have done wickedly, and have rebelled, even by departing from thy precepts and from thy judgments:"

Therefore, God took Prophet Daniel to such a high level in the Realm of the Spirit that he was able to see mightily into the future. God opened up Prophet Daniel's seer to see the times of tribulation when the antichrist shall set up his kingdom on this earth; and not only that but God showed him The Time when the King of Kings, and the Lord of Lords, the Ancient of Days shall reign. Daniel 7:9-11, "I beheld till the thrones were cast down, and the Ancient of days did sit, whose garment was white as snow, and the hair of his head like the pure wool: his throne was like the fiery flame, and his wheels as burning fire. A fiery stream issued and came forth from before him, and ten thousand times ten thousand stood before him: the judgment was set, and the books were opened. I beheld then because of the voice of the great words which the horn spake: I beheld even till the beast was slain, and his body destroyed, and given to the burning flame." Now, That Is Moving In Prophecy Of The Future!!!!! God was showing me that because Prophet Daniel's heart was totally for God and God's people, Jehovah God, My Father, withheld nothing from him. He gave His beloved, the Prophet, the past, the present, and the future. God opened up My Seer to Receive. Glory to God, Forever!!!

KNOWING THE ENEMY

When Jesus spoke the parable in Luke 14:31-33, He was saying not only do we need to know who our enemy is but we also need to be willing to face whatever comes our way. Luke 14:31-33 says, "Or what king, going to make war against another king, sitteth not down first, and consulteth whether he be able with ten thousand to meet him that cometh against him with twenty thousand? Or else, while the other is yet a great way off, he sendeth an ambassage, and desireth conditions of peace. So likewise, whosoever he be of you that forsaketh not all that he hath, he cannot be my disciple." When the Word tells you to make peace, I believe it means get in the presence of the Lord and get stronger so you are able to destroy all the works of the devil with the anointing. So, it is of utmost importance that we have our own personal relationship with Our God. We need to know God the Father, God the Son, and God the Holy Spirit. Otherwise, when we go to war, in the realm of the spirit, the enemy is going to want to cut your head off, especially if you are called to be or are already a Prophet of God. Remember, Jezebel, which represents a controlling spirit, was after Prophet Elijah in I Kings 19, and Herodias, Herod's wife, who had John the Baptist's head cut off because she hated that he had told her she was an adulterous woman in Mark 6:17-25. When you are moving in the realm of the spirit and God is using you to deliver His people, you have to be in tune to the voice of Your God and He has to be personal to you. The Word of God says in Exodus chapter 6 that God became a personal God, Jehovah, to Moses because he moved in deliverance. To Abraham, Isaac, and Jacob, He was God Almighty. Once you step into deliverance, He wants to become Jehovah to you. Exodus 6:3, "And I appeared unto Abraham, unto Isaac, and unto

Jacob, by the name of God Almighty, but by my name JEHOVAH was I not known to them." Remember, there are three voices: God's voice of which brings peace, our voice of which brings confusion, and the enemy's voice of which brings destruction. When we get into the Word of God and separate ourselves to really know Our God, He will become very personal. Like the Prophet Isaiah said in Isaiah 25:1, "O Lord, thou are my God,..." As we continue to build that relationship with Our God, we should be able to recognize His voice. John 10:27 says, "My sheep hear my voice, and I know them, and they follow me." Just as important, we need to know who are enemy is so we can keep from falling into his traps.

One of the biggest tactics of the enemy is to get us to gossip or listen to gossip. If we talk about someone, or listen to someone talking about others, we are defiled and have fallen from the grace of God, in accordance to the Word of God. Hebrews 12: 14, 15, "Follow peace with all men, and holiness, without which no man shall see the Lord: looking diligently lest any man fail of the grace of God; lest any root of bitterness springing up trouble you, and thereby many be defiled." Many years back, when I still had my secular job, I called a young woman while on my break, to see how she was doing. She began complaining about her husband. He can't do this, he always does that, etc., etc. Knowing my break was over I said, "I need to get back to work," and hung up. Inside of me, I heard the still small voice saying, "Call her back and get right." However, I reasoned in my mind that I would be late getting back to work, so I didn't call. This was on a Friday. By Sunday, while sitting on my bed trying to read the Word of God, I realized I was having trouble focusing and being able to read. I looked at my husband, who was sitting next to me, and I felt something inside of me that didn't like him. So, I calmly told him; "Hey, Honey, I am having trouble reading the Word of God and when I look at you something inside of me doesn't like you." He said, "Stop, and allow the Spirit of the Living God to remind you of where you opened the door for the enemy." When I did what my husband said, immediately the Spirit of God reminded me of listening to the gossip from the young woman. I picked up the phone, repented to her for listening to gossip; told her to please never do that again to anyone. I got right with the Lord and was able to enjoy my time with My Lord, reading the Word. Also, I want to warn you how the enemy brings gossip with the Religious Spirit; "Did you hear about so and so?" "Well, I'm just calling you so you can pray for them." Hang up on them!! Proverbs 18:7, 8 says, "A fool's mouth is his destruction, and his lips are the snare of his soul. The words of a talebearer are as wounds, and they go down into the innermost parts of the belly." If we are true Prophets and men and women of God, God, Himself will reveal what and who we need to pray for.

The Kingdom of God is Repentance! We need to understand that and apply that in every area of our lives. An illustration: Remember what Jesus said in Matthew 5:27, 28, "You have heard that it was said by them of old time, Thou shalt not commit adultery: but I say unto you, that whosoever looketh on a woman to lust after her hath committed adultery with her already in his heart." So, the first look is for free; the second look is going to cost you. The enemy plants a seed of adultery unless we repent. Notice if the enemy is able to plant a bad seed, he will not collect immediately. He waits till we are in a position of authority or step into the call of God for our lives and then he comes to destroy. An example in the Bible is in I Samuel chapter 25, when David's men had helped Nabal's shepherds in the field and David and his men were in need of food and supplies. David asked Nabal if he would supply for their needs. However, Nabal went against David and his men. When Abigail, Nabal's wife, heard of it she went out to calm the anger of David before he destroyed her and all her household. Now remember, she is a married woman; first in I Samuel 25:25, she talks bad about her husband. Then in I Samuel 25:31 when she says, "...but when the Lord shall have dealt well with my lord, then remember thine handmaid." The enemy planted a seed of adultery and later when David became King over all Israel, the enemy came to collect using Bathsheba. Read it in II Samuel chapter 11. This is why we need to learn to search our hearts daily and repent. Apostle Paul said it like this in Acts 24:16, "And herein do I exercise myself, to have always a conscience void of offense toward God, and toward men." God the Father hates sin, in fact, when we sin, He is ready to kill us but Jesus Christ, our mediator, who sits at His right hand, stands up and shows the Father His scars in His hands and side and says, "For this Reason I Died!" That is why when we make a mistake we need to run to Our God and get right. (I John 1:8, 9, 10 and I John 2:1, 2)

If your husband moves you, if your wife moves you, if your kids or anyone is able to move you, you have a door open for the enemy to attack. We have to allow Jesus Christ to be All in All in our lives. Many of us are looking for peace in our relationships here on earth. The only true Peace is JESUS. That means let Jesus fulfill every area in your heart and keep Him with you everywhere you go. When we do this, we will be able to follow what the Word says in Hebrews 12:14, "Follow peace with all men, without which no man shall see the Lord." It is up to us to follow peace by having Jesus with us everywhere we go. We will then be ready to slap the devil in his face when he comes at us, by speaking the Word of God.

Again, remember the enemy is an imitator. He is trying to plant bad seeds wherever he can. This is why it is so important that if the Jehovah witnesses or any other religious sect that does not acknowledge that Jesus is God comes to your door, kick them off your property because they are trying to subvert anyone who hears. The Bible says don't even say, "God Bless you" to them. Read it! II John, verses 9, 10, and 11; "Whosoever transgresseth, and abideth not in the doctrine of Christ, hath not God. He that abideth in the doctrine of Christ, he hath both the Father and the Son. If there come any unto you, and bring not this doctrine, receive him not into your house, neither bid him God speed. For he that biddeth him God speed is partaker of his evil deeds." One day everyone including satan and his demons will bow down and acknowledge that Jesus Christ is LORD! (Philippians 2:9)

In order to enter into the Kingdom of God we have to become as a child; Matthew 18:3, "And said, Verily I say unto you, except ye be converted, and become as little children, ye shall not enter into the kingdom of heaven." What God is showing us here is, forgiveness. When you take a toy from a child and they are upset, within seconds they forget about it and go on to something else. We need to learn to forgive from our hearts quickly and get back up and go again. If there is an area still bothering you from the past, you need deliverance from the spirit of bondage and from the tormenting spirits that continue to remind you. There is an illustration of how we put ourselves in prison. The tormenting spirits come when we don't forgive others. (Matthew 18:22-35) Forgive and receive forgiveness for we are not ignorant of the devil's devices. II Corinthians 2:10,

11, "To whom ye forgive any thing, I forgive also: for if I forgave any thing, to whom I forgave it, for your sakes forgave I it in the person of Christ; lest Satan should get an advantage of us: for we are not ignorant of his devices."

The religious spirit will try to keep someone from truly knowing Jesus and the Power of God, which is the Holy Spirit. Jesus, Himself told the Pharisees, the religious leaders, when they tried to accuse Him of casting out devils by Beelzebub that Satan cannot cast out Satan. Let us look at the scriptures: Matthew 12:24-29 says, "But when the Pharisees heard it, they said, this fellow doth not cast out devils, but by Beelzebub the prince of the devils. And Jesus knew their thoughts, and said unto them, "Every kingdom divided against itself is brought to desolation: and every city or house divided against itself shall not stand: And if Satan cast out Satan, he is divided against himself; how shall then his kingdom stand? And if I by Beelzebub cast out devils, by whom do your children cast them out? Therefore they shall be your judges. But if I cast out devils by the Spirit of God, then the kingdom of God is come unto you. Or else how can one enter into a strong man's house, and spoil his goods, except he first bind the strong man? And then he will spoil his house." There are several things to see through the words Jesus Christ spoke here. First of all, when Jesus said Satan cannot cast out Satan through this, we need to understand that we need to be walking in holiness, separated unto the Lord not only in our physical bodies but in our mind, will, and emotions. (I Thessalonians 5:23) If we ourselves are dealing with a spirit of lust or addictions, etc., we will not be able to cast it out of anyone else. The other thing that we should note in Jesus' words is how can we enter into a strong man's house and spoil his goods, except we first bind the strong man. If we don't know who the enemy is or who his strong men are, how can we bind them. This is the reason we need to know who our enemy is and in spite of contrary belief, it is not your husband, or your wife, or your brothers or sisters in Christ, etc; our enemy is not flesh and blood. Ephesians 6:12 says, "For we wrestle not against flesh and blood, but against principalities, against powers, against the rulers of the darkness of this world, against spiritual wickedness in high places." Jesus came to destroy the enemy and that's what He calls us to do. I John 3:8, "...For this purpose the Son of God was manifested, that he might destroy the works of the devil." Jesus was not omni-present when He was here; that is why He sent the Holy Spirit so we could do greater works. Because all of us being full of the Holy Spirit we can be doing the work of God in many places at once. And until Jesus ascended into heaven and sent His Holy Spirit no one was Born Again. Now that is a Great Work! (John 3:3-8)

Jehovah God, Almighty is a creator and we need to remember Satan is only an imitator. So, just like Jesus had twelve disciples, we believe God has shown us that Satan has twelve strong men. The difference is in God all things are good; there is no evil or shadow of turning. Satan tries to imitate but he twists, turns, and perverts everything to bring in destruction. In all this, God is involved. God wants us to choose to serve Him freely. Like the Word of God says in Proverbs 16:4, "The Lord hath made all things for himself: yea, even the wicked for the day of evil." We need to not only know who the enemy is but also to understand his tactics. Below is a list of the Strongmen and their roots according to what the Lord has shown us.

FEAR and all Roots of Fear (II Timothy 1:7, "For God hath not given us the spirit of fear; but of power, and of love, and of a sound mind.")

Tormented Heart	Sense Danger
Horror	Think Worst
Poverty	Heights
Worry	Shy
Cancer	Heart Attacks
Anxiety	Fear of Man
Inferiority	Fear of Future
Inadequacy	Fear of the Unknown
Tension	Fear of Failure
Stress	Incredibility
Timidity	Unbelief
Nightmares	Doubt

BONDAGE and all Roots of Bondage (Romans 8:15, "For you have not received the spirit of bondage again to fear; but ye have received the Spirit of adoption, whereby we cry, Abba, Father.")

All Compulsory Addictions	Anguish of Spirit
Cigarettes	Satanic Activity
Alcohol	Spiritual Blindness
Drugs	Prayerlessness
Lust	Abused Ambition
Unforgiveness	Bruised Ambition
Bitterness	Broken Ambition
Greed	Power
Cancer	Money
Bound	Adultery

JEALOUSY and all Roots of Jealousy (Numbers 5:14, "And the spirit of jealousy come upon him, and he be jealous of his wife, and she be defiled: or if the spirit of jealousy come upon him and he be jealous of his wife, and she be not defiled.")

Rage	Cruelty
Murder	Hate
Anger	Selfishness
Suspicion	Division
Competition	Wrath
Revenge	Envy
Restlessness	Offence

LYING and all Roots of Lying (II Chronicles 18:21, "And he said, I will go out, And be a lying spirit in the mouth of all his prophets. And the Lord said, Thou shalt entice him, and thou shalt also prevail: go out, and do even so.")

Lies	Critical Acclaim
Homosexuality	Tells loves you – Does not
Adultery	Vain Imagination
Fornication	Criticizes Man or Woman of God
Sodomy*	Nobody Satisfies Them
Profanity	Esteems Self High

Superstition	Wants Revenge
Divination	False Visions
Witchcraft	Isolates Self
Vanity	Insinuation
Hypocrisy	Driving Spirits
Strong Delusion	Vain Notations
Religious Spirit	Deception
Exaggeration	Little Lies

*Please note the definition of Sodomy as found in Webster's New Collegiate Dictionary. Sodomy: noncoital, especially anal or oral copulation with a member of the opposite sex. Copulation with a member of the same sex. This definition covers masturbation, anal or oral sex. These acts are demonic and need to be renounced and cast out.

FAMILIAR and all Roots of Familiar (I Samuel 28:7, "Then said Saul unto his servants, Seek me a woman that hath a familiar spirit, that I may go to her, and inquire of her. And his servants said to him, Behold, there is a woman that hath a familiar spirit at Endor.")

Occult	Smells
Fortune Telling	Music Beats
Horoscope	Incense
Astrology	Witch
New Age	Hypnosis
Divination of the Future	ESP TM
Demons	Psychic Ability
Sounds	Ouija Board

PERVERSION and all Roots of Perversion (Isaiah 19:14, "The Lord hath mingled a perverse spirit in the midst thereof: and they have caused Egypt to err in every work thereof, as a drunken man staggereth in his in his vomit.")

Twisted Word	Sex Troubles
Turn the Truth	Homosexuality
Doctrinal Error	Lust

Wrong Teaching	Pervert the Gospel
Hatred of God	Rebellion
Wounded Spirit	Hate
Self Lovers	Error
Oral Sex	Masturbation
Lasciviousness	Bestiality

HEAVINESS and all Roots of Heaviness (Isaiah 61:3, "To appoint unto them that mourn in Zion, to give unto them beauty for ashes, the oil of joy for mourning, the garment of praise for the spirit of heaviness; that they might be called trees of righteousness, the planting of the Lord, that he might be glorified.")

Self Pity	Mourning
Rejection	Troubled
Sorrow	Gluttony
Sadness	Idolatry
Hopelessness	Devil is God
Grief	Depression
Loneliness	Abandonment
Gloominess	Burden
Despair	Disgust
Discouragement	Crying

WHOREDOM and all Roots of Whoredom (Hosea 4:12, "My people ask counsel at their stocks, and their staff declareth unto them: for the spirit of whoredoms hath caused them to err, and they have gone a whoring from under their God.")

Unclean	Love of Money
Foul	Love of Food
Idolatry	Pornography
Homosexuality	All Sexual Sin
Fornication	Emotional Weakness
Prostitution	Unequally Yoked
Adultery	Poverty
Love of World	Lust

INFIRMITY and all Roots of Infirmity (Luke 13:11, "And, behold, there was a woman which had a spirit of infirmity eighteen years, and was bowed together, and could in no wise lift up herself.")

All Sickness	Fever
Cancer	Weakness
Heart Problems	Hunchback
Asthma	Lungs
Arthritis	Bones
Sinus	Muscles
Ears	Eyes
Viruses	Headaches
Cold	Insomnia
Blood	

DUMB/DEAF and all Roots of Dumb/Deaf (Mark 9:25, "When Jesus saw that the people came running together, he rebuked the foul spirit, saying unto him., Thou dumb and deaf spirit, I charge thee, come out of him, and enter no more into him.")

Suicide	Tearing
Convulsions	Foaming of the Mouth
Epilepsy	Pining Away
Seizures	Can't Function
Schizophrenia	Death
Lunatic	Distraction
Insane	Self Destruction
Inner Ear Disease	Generational Curses
Blindness	Eye Diseases
Dumbness	Deafness

ANTICHRIST and all Roots of Antichrist (I John 4:3, "And every spirit that confesseth not that Jesus Christ is come in the flesh is not of God; and this is that spirit of antichrist, whereof ye have heard that it should come; and even now already is in the world.")

Legalism	Appoint Selves
Blasphemies	Against Christ
Controlling Spirit	Attempts Christ's Place

Manipulation

Opposing Man of God
Substitute the Blood
Persecute the Saints
Speak Against the Gifts
Condemnation

Suppress Ministries
(Keeping you from the call of
God in your life.)
Humanism
Atheism
New Age
Homosexual (Daniel 11:37)

PRIDE and all Roots of Pride (Proverbs 16:18, 19, "Pride goeth before destructtion and an haughty spirit before a fall. Better it is to be of an humble spirit with the lowly, than to divide the spoil with the proud.")

Stubbornness
Gossip
Controlling Spirit
Arrogance
Self Righteousness
Contention
Wrathful
Mockery
Shame

Scorner
Egotistic
Haughtiness
Proud Vanity
Dictatorial
Prejudice
Criticism
Importance
Manipulation

If we understand the ways of Our God and know that He only wants good for us, we can rejoice no matter what trial or tribulation comes our way. The Word of God says in Psalms 37:23, "The steps of a good man are ordered by the Lord and he delighteth in his way." I am saying all this because God will use the enemy to get us to the next level in the realm of the spirit. Let us look at the book of Job starting in chapter 1:6-12; it was God who said to Satan, "Have you noticed my servant, Job. In other words, God had to smack Satan on the back of the head to get his attention to go after Job. Why, because God wants us to go from glory to glory. I also want you to notice in verses 6 and 7 what it says; "Now there was a day when the sons of God came to present themselves before the Lord, and Satan came also among them. And the Lord said unto Satan, Whence comest thou? Then Satan answered the Lord and said, "From going to and fro in the earth, and from walking up and down in it." See, when Adam sinned against God, Satan not only had dominion over the second heaven (where principalities are) but Adam, by sinning, gave him dominion over the first heaven. That is why Satan answered from going to and fro in the earth and from walking up and down in it, because he had dominion over the first and the second heaven. God illustrates the three heavens to us when He told Noah to build the Ark having three stories in Genesis 6:16 and again through what the Apostle Paul says in II Corinthians 12:2 where the Apostle Paul talks about himself being taken up into the third heaven. (The third heaven being the throne of God.) The Word of God says "I knew a man in Christ above fourteen years ago, (whether in the body, I cannot tell; or whether out of the body, I cannot tell: God knoweth;) such an one caught up to the third heaven." So, you see in the book of Job how God had to get Satan's attention to go against Job. Also, notice that Satan bragged about Job. Read verse 8, 9 and 10, "And the Lord said unto Satan, Hast thou considered my servant Job, that there is none like him in the earth, a perfect and an upright man, one that feareth God, and escheweth evil? Then Satan answered the Lord, and said, Doth Job fear God for nought? Hast not thou made an hedge about him, and about his house, and about all that he hath on every side? Thou hast blessed the work of his hands, and his substance is increased in the land." How many of us are living and going all out for the Lord Jesus that the enemy would be bragging about us before Our God? Let us look at the rest of the conversation to see how God used the enemy to bring the tribulations into Job's life. Read verses 11 and 12, "But put forth thine hand now, and touch all that he hath, and he will curse thee to thy face. And the Lord said unto Satan, Behold, all that he hath is in thy power; only upon himself put not forth thine hand. So Satan went forth from the presence of the Lord." Once Job passed the test, he went higher in the realm of the spirit where again Satan couldn't touch him. Then again in Job chapter 2:1-7 God wants Job to go even higher in the realm of the spirit so He brings Job to Satan's attention once more. We need to understand in the kingdom of God we don't flunk a test, we just keep getting to take it over and over again until we pass. In this case, Job passed the first test and God wanted him to go higher and higher in the realm of the spirit.

Remember, knowing the ways of our enemy is important. Satan is an imitator and he wants to build his own kingdom. The Word of God says in John 10:10, "The thief cometh not, but for to steal, and to kill, and to destroy; I am come that they might have life, and that they might have it more abundantly." We, as born again Christians, need to know the authority the Lord Jesus has given to us when He became the second Adam. Read in I Corinthians 15:45, "And so it is written, the first man Adam was made a living soul; the last Adam was made a quickening spirit." When Jesus Christ died on the cross, Jesus kicked Satan out of the first heaven. The dominion over the first heaven, that is here on earth, was given back to the born again Christians. John 12:31, "Now is the judgment of this world: now shall the prince of this world be cast out." According to the Word of God when we become born again Satan cannot touch us. I John 5:18, "We know that whosoever is born of God sinneth not; but he that is begotten of God keepeth himself, and that wicked one toucheth him not." However, when we don't know our authority and/or when we open the door for the enemy with anger, unforgiveness, bitterness, etc, etc, that is how Satan begins to build his kingdom. Let us look at what happened to Judas Iscariot's life. Read John 13:2 says, "And supper being ended, the devil having now put into the heart of Judas Iscariot, Simon's son, to betray him;" We need to notice, first of all, Judas was right in the presence of Jesus Christ Himself and he opened the door for the enemy. Many of us think just because we go to church or because we are reading the Word of God that the enemy can't touch us. This is not true; because if we open the door of our hearts for greed, lust, offence, or any of the enemies attacks, and don't repent, Satan puts his foot right there to keep the door open so he can establish his kingdom. Other people say, "The blood of Jesus covers me." Again, we need to remember even in the Old Testament in the book of Exodus during the Passover time God warned the Israelites not to come out from the door where the blood of the Lamb had covered it so that the spirit of death could not affect them. Read it in Exodus 12:22, "And ye shall take a bunch of hyssop, and dip it in the blood that is in the basin, and strike the lintel and the two side posts with the blood that is in the basin, and none of you shall go out at the door of his house until the morning." The blood of Jesus does not cover us if we open the door for the enemy. In John 12:4-6 we read how Judas Iscariot already had the door of his heart open for greed; when Mary of Bethany had poured the ointment on Jesus feet, Judas Iscariot made a comment about how this could have been sold to the poor. John 12:6 says, "This he said, not that he cared for the poor; but because he was a thief, and had the bag, and bare what was put therein." God was showing us here, that not only the poor can have a thieving spirit but even the rich for Judas Iscariot came from a wealthy family, Simon, the Pharisee was his father. (John 12:4) We need to see how Satan is not satisfied with a person just having one or two unclean spirits, he is looking to fill a person so he can establish his kingdom. Acts 5:3 says, "But Peter said, Ananias, why had Satan filled thine heart to lie to the Holy Ghost, and to keep back part of the price of the land?" Notice it says, "filled thine heart." This is what the enemy is trying to do. In this case, where Ananias and his wife, Sapphira, allowed the enemy to fill their hearts then their lives were taken from them. The same with Judas Iscariot in John 13:27, Satan entered into Judas Iscariot's heart completely when he didn't repent and turn from his ways. John 13:27 says, "And after the sop Satan entered into him. Then said Jesus unto him, that thou doest, do quickly." Satan is not satisfied until he establishes his kingdom in someone. That is why we need to understand the kingdom of God is all about repentance and getting back up again.

When you fall down the enemy is trying to keep you down by putting the spirit of shame or the spirit of condemnation on you. This is why it is of utmost importance in our spiritual walk to know who the enemy is!! I am going to show you through the life of our beautiful beloved Apostle Peter how the enemy will try to keep you down with shame and condemnation. We all know how zealous Apostle Peter was for the Lord. In his zeal, he made a lot of mistakes. When he saw Jesus walking on the water I believe he was telling Jesus I want to do that call me _____. When he kept his eyes on Jesus he was okay, but when he put his eyes on the situation, just like we do when we focus on the trial or tribulation, he sunk. (Matthew 14:22-33) Then in Matthew 16:13-19 when Jesus asked "Whom do men say that I the Son of man am?" And they said, some say that thou art John the Baptist: some, Elias; and others, Jeremias, or one of the prophets." And Simon Peter answered and said, "Thou art the Christ, the Son of the living God." And Jesus answered and said unto him, "Blessed art thou Simon Barjona: for flesh and blood hath not revealed it unto thee but my Father which is in heaven." When Jesus glorified what God the Father had revealed to Peter, I believe the spirit of pride entered into him because just a few verses later Matthew 16:20-23, Jesus began explaining to the disciples how He must go to Jerusalem and that he would be beaten and killed. Apostle Peter began to rebuke Our Master. As Jesus looked at him and the other disciples He said, "Get thee behind me Satan....". Can you imagine how Peter felt being rebuked in front of the other disciples and allowing his mouth to be used by Satan. Then in Matthew 17:1-8 on the Mount of Transfiguration fear came upon Peter and he said let us make another way to God by building tents for Moses and Elijah. God the Father had to speak to correct Peter that JESUS is the Only Way and to listen to Him. Again in Matthew 18, obviously Peter had something against his brother Andrew because he asked Jesus how many times must I forgive my brother. Probably Andrew couldn't understand why Peter was always with Jesus. When Peter asked Jesus how many times must I forgive He told him seventy times seven; now that's a lot of forgiving. Then again in Matthew 17:24-27 when the tax collectors tried to plant a seed in Peter's heart against Jesus not paying taxes Jesus stopped Peter before he could open his mouth and get into trouble by asking him who should pay tribute their own children or strangers. However, you will see Jesus said nevertheless so that we don't offend them he sent Peter out saying you go do my work and I will provide. Go fishing for souls and I will supply the money. Then when Peter was with Jesus in the Garden of Gethsemane he cut off the young man's ear. (Matthew 26:51) I believe Peter thought this guy doesn't have ears to hear what the Holy Ghost has to say so he doesn't need his ear. (Ha!) However, Jesus looked at Peter, healed the man's ear and I believe Jesus was telling Peter wait until you're full of the Holy Ghost before you discern who doesn't have ears to hear. Peter was very impetuous. Then when Jesus told the disciples they would all be offended because of him; of course, Peter said not me. (Matthew 26:31-35) As you know, Peter denied knowing Jesus three times. Peter made many many mistakes just like all of us. However, Jesus knew this and even warned Peter telling him, "Simon, Simon, behold, Satan hath desired to have you, that he may sift you as wheat." But look what Jesus says to encourage Peter: But I have prayed for thee, that thy faith fail not: and when thou art converted, strengthen thy brethren. (Luke 22:31, 32) The spirit of shame and condemnation was so heavy on Peter that when Jesus had arose from the dead an angel of God told Mary and the other women with her to "Go tell the disciples and Peter that he goeth before you into Galilee." (Mark 16:7) Again in John 21:3-19 you can see Peter having gone back to fishing was naked which represents shame and no covering. (Read verse 7) However, when Jesus called out to them, Peter realized it was time to put on his fishers coat; in other words he knew it was time to put on his Apostolic Mantle and jump in head first into the water (The Word of God). No matter what we have done we need to repent and go on with Jesus. Like Apostle Paul said in Philippians 3:13, 14 "Brethren, I count not myself to have apprehended: but this one thing I do, forgetting those things which are behind, and reaching forth unto those things which are before, I press toward the mark for the prize of the high calling in God in Christ Jesus."

When Jesus spoke to all the churches in the book of Revelations chapters 2 and 3; to every church He said, "And he that overcometh,…" Read Revelations 2:7, "….To him that overcometh will I give to eat of the tree of life,…", Revelations 2:11, "…He that overcometh shall not be hurt of the second death.", Revelations 2:17, "…To him that overcometh will I give to eat of the hidden manna, and will give him a white stone…", Revelations 2:26, "And he that overcometh, and keepeth my works unto the end, to him will I give power over the nations:", Revelations 3:5, "He that overcometh, the same shall be clothed in white raiment; and I will not blot out his name out of the book of life,…", Revelations 3:12, "Him that overcometh will I make a pillar in the temple of my God,…", Revelations 3:21, "To him that overcometh will I grant to sit with me in my throne,…" The key to the kingdom of God is spoken to us in II Chronicles 7:14, "If my people, which are called by my name, shall humble themselves;" which means going to one another whether it be our husbands, wives, kids, brothers and sisters in Christ, whomever and asking them to forgive us. Then go to the Lord in prayer to ask for forgiveness. Many of us don't humble ourselves to one another, we just ask God to forgive us. However, if you read Matthew 5:23, 24, "Therefore if thou bring thy gift to the altar, and there rememberest that thy brother hath ought against thee: leave there thy gift before the altar, and go thy way; first be reconciled to thy brother, and then come and offer thy gift." God is telling us that we can't buy God with our gifts. He wants us to stop praying, get up and go get right with each other first and then come to Him and He will hear our prayers. II Chronicles 7:14 continued; "….and pray, and seek my face, and turn from their wicked ways, then will I hear from heaven, and will forgive their sin, and will heal their land." Then when we ask God to forgive us, we need to seek His face and by being filled with the Word of God we will be able to turn from our wicked ways. What God is trying to tell each and every one of us is that He knows that there will be times when we will make mistakes but we need to do what the Word of God says; humble ourselves, pray, seek His face, and turn from our wicked ways. Condemnation and shame are not of God; Romans 8:1, "There is therefore now no condemnation to them which are in Christ Jesus, who walk not after the flesh, but after the Spirit." Conviction and Repentance is the Way of Our God. Don't let the enemy keep you down. Hebrews 10:39, "But we are not of them who draw back unto perdition; but of them that believe to the saving of the soul." I am going to share with you a story I heard: There was a farmer who had a donkey and he fell in a deep well in the neighbor's yard. The neighbor told the farmer and the farmer said, "Well the donkey is old and I don't need him anymore you can have the donkey." The neighbor told the farmer, "Well I don't want the donkey and I don't use the well anymore so help me just fill in the well." So the farmer threw a pile of dirt on the donkey and the donkey shook it off. Then the neighbor threw a pile of dirt on the donkey and again the donkey shook it off. This continued over and over and as the donkey shook it off he was raised all the way to the surface and then just walked away. This is how we need to be. "Shake it Loose" and go on with the things of the Lord.

APOSTOLIC TEACHINGS

Revelations of the Word of God

Many Prophets are able to move in the teaching anointing and to teach the Word of God because they receive the revelations of the Word of God according to Ephesians 3:1-5. In Our Ministry, that the Lord blessed us with, we teach and train up everyone to know how to evangelize, how to preach, teach, prophesy, how to lead someone into the kingdom of God, how to go into the hearts of people and how to move in the prophetic no matter what calling they have. We also continually pray for each one of them so they can carry and move in the anointing of the Lord. It is by the laying on of hands according to II Timothy 1:6, "Wherefore I put thee in remembrance that thou stir up the gift of God, which is in thee by the putting on of my hands," that the gifts of God are imparted. Also, in Deuteronomy 34:9, when Moses laid hands on Joshua, Moses imparted the anointing to Joshua. "And Joshua the son of Nun was full of the spirit of wisdom for Moses had laid his hands upon him: and the children of Israel hearkened unto him, and did as the Lord commanded Moses." This section is to give you a few small Apostolic teachings that you too can learn and allow God to activate the teaching anointing in your life. We need to be teaching the Word of God, not theology or doctrines of man. According to Acts 2:42, "And they continued stedfastly in the Apostles' doctrine and fellowship, and in breaking of bread, and in prayers." Below are a few Apostolic teachings full of the Word of God and the revelations of His Word. God is not looking for pretty preachers or a good sermon, God is looking for the impartation of His Word for his people.

If we desire to have the revelations of the Word of God revealed to us, pray these scriptures and ask the Lord to open up your eyes and teach you. Pray I John 2:27 over your life, "But the anointing which ye have received of him abideth in you, and ye need not that any man teach you: but as the same anointing teacheth you of all things, and is truth, and is no lie, and even as it hath taught you, ye shall abide in him." Ask Him to be your Teacher. This does not mean you cannot receive or be taught by man, this only means that while you are spending your time and searching the scriptures that the Spirit of the Living God will give you understanding. Pray Ephesians 1:17-20, "That the God of our Lord Jesus Christ, the Father of glory, may give unto you the spirit of wisdom and revelation in the knowledge of him. The eyes of your understanding being enlightened; that ye may know what is the hope of his calling, and what the riches of the glory of his inheritance in the saints. And what is the exceeding greatness of his power to us-ward who believe, according to the working of his mighty power, which he wrought in Christ, when he raised him from the dead, and set him at his own right hand in the heavenly places." Praying this prayer God can open up your spiritual eyes to see and receive the revelations of the Word of God of which are life giving. In Revelations 4:6-11 when it speaks about the four beast full of eyes before and behind and the twenty four elders and the angels in heaven surrounding the throne of God and all they can say is: "Holy, Holy, Holy, Lord God Almighty, which was, and is, and is to come." See every time they look on the Gloriousness of Our God, The Beauty of His Holiness, The Awesomeness of His Power, I believe they are receiving new revelations of His Bigness and all they can say is, "HOLY, HOLY, HOLY." That is how it should be when we are spending time in the presence of Our God reading His Word; we should be receiving revelations upon revelations and saying, "HOLY, HOLY, HOLY, LORD GOD, ALMIGHTY."

Teaching #1

The Lover of My Soul

Through the Word of God, I am going to show you two women who not only liked Jesus Christ, who not only loved Jesus Christ, but they were in love with Jesus Christ, the Lover of their souls. See, when

you like someone or love someone you still do t\
you are In Love with someone you don't want to\
them. That's how we need to be with Our Lord,\
The Lover of Our Soul. We need to be like the w\
of Song of Solomon 3:1-4, "By night on my bed I s\
my soul loveth: I sought him, but I found him not.\
and go about the city in the streets, and in the broad \   …11 seek\
him whom my soul loveth: I sought him but I found nim not. The watchmen that go about the city found me: to whom I said, Saw ye him whom my soul loveth? It was but a little that I passed from them, but I found him whom my soul loveth: I held him, and would not let him go, until I had brought him into my mother's house, and into the chamber of her that conceived me." This woman not only liked Jesus, she not only loved Jesus, but this woman was in love with Jesus Christ. She had a hunger and a passion for the Word of God. The Word says this woman woke up early in the morning when it was still dark outside to seek the Lover of Her Soul. How many of us are rising early, spending time in the Word of God, giving Him the first fruits of our day? The Word of God says blessed is he who seeks me early; He loves those that seek Him early and those that seek Him early shall find Him. When she found him not, she rose up quickly to search the house to see where the Lover of Her Soul had gone. She went from the bedroom, to the bathroom, to the living room; she had a big house and she went throughout the house searching for The Lover of Her Soul. For us this means that we need to search our hearts to see where we have opened the door; was it for offence, bitterness, unforgiveness, gossip or why was it that the Lover of Her Soul was not there. Like it says in Psalm 4:4, "…commune with your own heart upon your bed, and be still." This woman didn't give up she searched in every room of her house. When she knew her heart was right with the Lord, she still did not give up the search for the Lover of Her Soul. There are times when we feel like we are in the desert; God is using those times to prove our character like the Word says in Deuteronomy 8:2, "And thou shalt remember all the way which the Lord thy God led thee these forty years in the wilderness, to humble thee, and to prove thee, to know what was in thine heart, whether thou wouldest keep his commandments, or no." See God wants to make sure that all the anger, bitterness, resentment and everything that is not of the Lord is out of us so we can stand on

rd. When this woman couldn't find the Lover of Her Soul in her
se she ran into the streets asking everyone, "Have you seen Him?
Have you seen the Lover of My Soul?" But it says she found Him not.
This woman kept seeking for Him. As she was searching, she came
across the watchmen and asked him, "Have you seen the Lover of My
Soul?" A watchmen is a Prophet of God according to Ezekiel 3:17,
"Son of man, I have made thee a watchman unto the house of Israel:
therefore hear the word at my mouth, and give them warning from
me." Because this Prophet hadn't been spending time in the Word or
worshipping the Lord, he wasn't ready in season and out of season. How
many of us are giving God His time? Ten percent of our day belongs to
God; that means approximately two hours and forty minutes. If we're
not giving our time to our God we are robbing Him. When someone
comes to us for that word of comfort, edification or exhortation we
won't have it, just like the watchmen when the woman came to him.
I believe this watchman saw the love and passion this woman had that
he probably asked her, "When you find Him, please tell me." This
woman was so in love with the Lover of Her Soul that she continued
on until she found Him and then she fell at His feet and grabbed Him
and wouldn't let Him go, until she brought Him back to her mother's
house. How many of us are like that when we find Jesus, we fall at
His feet worshipping Him and won't let Him go? When we have that
love and that passion for Our Lord Jesus we want to share Him with
everyone just as this woman did.

There is another woman that I want to show you through the Word
of God that had this same passion and love and she too didn't stop
searching until she found the Lover of Her Soul. Her name was Mary
Magdalene. Let's read John 20:1-17, "The first day of the week cometh
Mary Magdalene early, when it was yet dark, unto the sepulchre, and
seeth the stone taken away from the sepulchre. Then she runneth, and
cometh to Simon Peter, and to the other disciple, whom Jesus loved, and
saith unto them, "They have taken away the Lord out of the sepulchre,
and we know not where they have laid him." Peter therefore went
forth, and that other disciple, and came to the sepulchre. So they ran
both together: and the other disciple did outrun Peter, and came first
to the sepulchre. And he stooping down, and looking in, saw the linen
clothes lying; yet went he not in. Then cometh Simon Peter following
him, and went into the sepulchre, and seeth the linen clothes lie, and

the napkin, that was about his head, not lying with the linen clothes, but wrapped together in a place by itself. Then went in also that other disciple, which came first to the sepulchre, and he saw, and believed. For as yet they knew not the scripture, that He must rise again from the dead. Then the disciples went away again unto their own home. But Mary stood without at the sepulchre weeping: and as she wept, she stooped down, and looked into the sepulchre, and seeth two angels in white sitting, the one at the head, and the other at the feet, where the body of Jesus had lain. And they say unto her, "Woman, why weepest thou?" She said unto them, "Because they have taken away my Lord, and I know not where they have laid him." And when she had thus said, she turned herself back, and saw Jesus standing, and knew not that it was Jesus. Jesus saith unto her, "Woman, why weepest thou? Whom seekest thou?" She, supposing him to be the gardener, saith unto him, "Sir, if thou have borne him hence, tell me where thou has laid him, and I will take him away." Jesus saith unto her, "Mary," She turned herself, and saith unto him, "Rabboni," which is to say, Master. Jesus saith unto her, "Touch me not; for I am not yet ascended to my Father: but go to my brethren, and say unto them, I ascend unto my Father, and your Father; and to my God, and your God." Mary Magdalene was so in Love with Jesus Christ that as it says in the Word she got up early to seek Him; while it was still dark outside. Mary went to go find the Lover of Her Soul. Again, how many of us are like this, rising early to seek Him or is it that when the dog needs to go out early in the morning we get up and let him out but when the Spirit of the Living God wakes us up to spend time with Him we hit the snooze button and go back to sleep? When Mary Magdalene got to the sepulchre she saw that the Lover of Her Soul was not there so she ran back to the other disciples to ask them, "Have you seen the Lover of My Soul?" When Peter and John heard this, they too ran to the sepulchre. Notice how it says that John outran Peter, but John stopped at the door and looked in. See, this is how many of us are. When it comes to the things of God; we are waiting for our husbands or our wives to step into their call before we go forward. But Peter didn't stop; he went head first into the sepulchre. I believe because Peter was an awesome example John went in too. What God is telling us is, if we go all out for the Lord, if we are awesome examples for our families, they will also want to seek the Lord. The Word specifically mentions that the napkin from

Jesus' head was folded and separated from the other linen clothes that had been on His body. Jesus was trying to leave them a message. In those days the Jewish people had a custom that when they came to your home to eat and liked the food and the company, they would fold their napkins neatly and set it to the side....meaning they were coming back. The message Jesus was giving us is that He was coming back for us to sup with us. Glory to God, Forever! Peter and John were excited when they saw this but they went back again to have a conference, but not Mary. This woman was looking for the Lover of Her Soul and she wasn't going to stop until she found Him. She sat outside the sepulchre weeping, longing to know who and where they had taken the Lover of Her Soul. She looked back into the sepulchre and as she did she saw two angels. Mary was a Prophet of God. She was able to move in the realm of the spirit and able to see the angels. I believe Mary thought seeing the folded napkin is good, seeing the angels is awesome, but this woman wasn't going to give up until she found the Lover of Her Soul. You can almost hear her asking the angels, "Do you know where they have taken Him?" When she turned her head back, she saw someone standing there supposing him to be the gardener. I believe because her eyes were so welled up with tears and because she was still looking for Jesus Christ of Nazareth, that is, Jesus Christ in the flesh, instead of Jesus Christ the First Born, the Holy One, that Mary didn't recognize Him. Mary asked Him, Where have they taken Him, do you know where He is? We need to remember that when Jesus Christ died on the cross He was naked but when He came back He came back as Our High Priest clothed with His new garments because He now is Jesus Christ, the first born, the Son of the Living God. And when Jesus said her name, "Mary," she knew this was Him. She knew this was the Lover of Her Soul. Now look at the Bigness of Our God; look at what Jesus said to her......He told her not to touch Him because He had not yet ascended to the Father. What God is trying to show us is that if we are like these women that are so in love with the Lord, seeking His face that He will stop His plans. He stopped His ascent to heaven. He will do whatever it takes to commune with us when we seek Him with all of our heart. Jesus stopped his ascent from going from the center of the earth where Abraham and all that awaited for the Messiah were to heaven because of this one woman's cry. Are we seeking The Lover of Our Soul like this? Fall in love with Jesus Christ, The Lover of Your

Soul, The Word of God. Have that passion that no one can stop you from being with Him!!

Teaching # 2

Having Soul Ties in Our Lives

Many of us know that Prophet Samuel was a powerful Prophet of God that God used mightily. God used this Prophet so mightily that the Lord didn't allow any of his words to fall to the ground. I Samuel 3:19: "And Samuel grew, and the Lord was with him and did let none of his words fall to the ground." In other words, because Prophet Samuel was so in tune with the Lord that everything Prophet Samuel spake came to pass. God showed Prophet Samuel things before they happened and revealed the hearts of people to him. Prophet Samuel had even told Saul when he came into his presence stay here tonight and tomorrow I will tell you everything that is in your heart. I Samuel 9:19: "And Samuel answered Saul, and said, I am the seer: go up before me unto the high place; for ye shall eat with me today and tomorrow I will let thee go, and will tell thee all that is in thine heart." This Prophet was used so powerfully by God that he could tell you the past, the present and the future. I Samuel 10:1-4: "Then Samuel took a vial of oil, and poured it upon his head, and kissed him, and said, Is it not because the Lord hath anointed thee to be captain over his inheritance? When thou art departed from me today, then thou shalt find two men by Rachel's sepulchre in the border of Benjamin at Zelzah; and they will say unto thee, the asses which thou wentest to seek are found: and, lo, thy father hath left the care of the asses, and sorroweth for you, saying, what shall I do for my son? Then shalt thou go on forward from thence, and thou shalt come to the plain of Tabor, and there shall meet thee three men going up to God to Bethel, one carrying three kids, and another carrying three loaves of bread, and another carrying a bottle of wine: and they will salute thee, and give thee two loaves of bread; which thou shalt receive of their hands." Prophet Samuel had told Saul the past of how he knew that Saul had been looking for his father's asses, the present that he was anointed to be King over Israel, and the future that when Saul left the presence of the Prophet he would meet two men to give him the news about the asses and from there he would then meet three men and he told them what they were carrying and what they would give him. Now, that is an awesome Prophet of God. However, what I want all of us to see here is that because the Prophet Samuel had been with King Saul for about forty years he had a soul tie with him. Let us read here in I Samuel 16:1-13 to see how much a soul tie affects a Prophet's life and how it affects their hearing and seeing in the realm of the spirit. "And the Lord said unto Samuel, How long wilt thou mourn for Saul, seeing I have rejected him from reigning over Israel? Fill thine horn with oil, and go, I will send thee to Jesse the Bethlehemite: for I have provided me a king among his sons." And Samuel said, "How can I go if Saul hear it, he will kill me." And the Lord said, "Take an heifer with thee, and say, I am come to sacrifice to the Lord. And call Jesse to the sacrifice, and I will shew thee what thou shalt do: and thou shalt anoint unto me him whom I name unto thee." And Samuel did that which the Lord spake, and came to Bethlehem. And the elders of the town trembled at his coming, and said, "Comest thou peaceably?" And he said, "Peaceably: I am come to sacrifice unto the Lord: sanctify yourselves, and come with me to the sacrifice." And he sanctified Jesse and his sons, and called them to the sacrifice. And it came to pass, when they were come, that he looked on Eliab, and said, Surely the Lord's anointed is before him. But the Lord said unto Samuel, "Look not on his countenance, or on the height of his stature; because I have refused him for the Lord seeth not as man seeth; for man looketh on the outward appearance, but the Lord looketh on the heart." Then Jesse called Abinadab, and made him pass before Samuel. And he said, "Neither hath the Lord chosen this." Then Jesse made Shammah to pass by. And he said, "Neither hath the Lord chosen this." Again, Jesse made seven of his sons to pass before Samuel. And Samuel said unto Jesse, "The Lord hath not chosen these." And Samuel said unto Jesse, "Are here all thy children?" And he said, "There remaineth yet the youngest, and behold, he keepeth the sheep." And Samuel said unto Jesse, "Send and fetch him; for we will not sit down till he come hither." And he sent, and brought him in. Now he was ruddy and withal of a beautiful countenance, and goodly to look to. And the Lord said, "Arise, anoint him: for this is he." Then Samuel took the horn of oil, and anointed him in the midst of his brethren: and the spirit of the Lord came upon David from that day forward. So Samuel rose up, and went to Ramah." Here was Prophet Samuel crying out and mourning for Saul because God had rejected him as being King over Israel. Prophet Samuel had cried out all night long for Saul. I Samuel 15:11, "It repenteth me that I have set up Saul to be king: for he is turned back from following me, and hath not performed my commandments." And it grieved Samuel; and he cried unto the Lord all night." It is not wrong for us to cry out and pray for a man or woman of God that has fallen out of the presence of the Lord but when God speaks that is it. The Lord said to Prophet Samuel how long are you going to mourn for Saul, enough is enough I have rejected him because of his rebellion and now I have a mission for you. But because Prophet Samuel had a soul tie with King Saul he had opened the door for the enemy so when God wanted to send him out on a mission the powerful Prophet Samuel had fear. Prophet Samuel said if I go Saul will kill me. According to II Timothy 1:7, "For God hath not given us the spirit of fear; but of power, and of love, and of a sound mind." When we open the door for fear, faith is not there and faith is the only thing that pleases God according to Hebrews 11:6, "But without faith it is impossible to please him; for he that cometh to God must believe that he is, and that he is a rewarder of them that diligently seek him." So God sent Prophet Samuel forth to Jesse's house to anoint the one God had chosen. When Prophet Samuel entered the town look at what the people said, "Are you coming in peace?" Prophet Samuel was known throughout all Israel as a powerful Prophet of God and people feared him. Just like the Word of God says in Deuteronomy 28:10, "And all people of the earth shall see that thou art called by the name of the Lord; and they shall be afraid of thee." How many of us are separated for the Lord and being used by God so powerfully that people tremble because of the presence of the Lord in our lives? Jesse and his family, like many of the people of God, sit around. They've been in church 5, 10, 15 and some 20 years waiting for the things of God. When God sends us on a mission for one person, God still wants not only that person be touched by God, but that everyone's life that we come in contact be effected. However, because Prophet Samuel had a soul tie he couldn't hear or see clearly from the Lord, this kept everyone that was in Jesse's house from receiving a Word or a Touch from God. What God is telling each and every one of us is that if your husband is in your heart, if your wife is in your heart, if your kids, or anyone or anything is in your heart besides Jesus Christ, these are idols in your heart. You will not be able to be used by God in the magnitude that God wants to use you. And God also says to have no other gods before Him. Notice that when Eliab the eldest son came in front of Prophet Samuel he said this must be the one the Lord has chosen. God had to stop him. God had to speak to the Prophet and let him know that man looks at the outward appearance but God is looking at our hearts. This is why we need to know each other by the spirit and not in the flesh. Jesse's sons Abinadab and Shammah then passed by and the Prophet said God has not chosen these either. Because Prophet Samuel had opened the door for the enemy instead of going into Jesse's house and giving that word of comfort, edification, or exhortation to David's brothers I believe not only were they discouraged but they also opened the door for jealousy toward David and this affected their lives later. After all the brothers had passed by, Prophet Samuel asked Jesse if there were anymore. Notice David wasn't just sitting around waiting for someone to tell him what to do; he was out doing what he was suppose to be doing. He was watching over the sheep. That is what we need to be doing, showing ourselves approved and being our brothers' keeper. When David came in front of Samuel, the Lord spoke right away and said, "Arise, anoint him for this is the one." So you can see because of a soul tie instead of going in and having an affect on all ten of them, David was the only one touched. We need to have only Jesus in our hearts so God can use us powerfully for His Glory!!

Teaching #3

The Gospel is Simple

Through the Word of God, I am going to show you the simplicity of Preaching the Gospel of Jesus Christ. Let's begin reading in II Kings 5:1-4, "Now Naaman, captain of the host of the king of Syria, was a great man with his master, and honourable, because by him the Lord had given deliverance unto Syria: he was also a mighty man in valour, but he was a leper. And the Syrians had gone out by companies, and had brought away captive out of the land of Israel a little maid; and she waited on Naaman's wife. And she said unto her mistress, Would God my lord were with the prophet that is in Samaria! For he would recover him of his leprosy. And one went in, and told his lord, saying, Thus and thus said the maid that is of the land of Israel." Naaman was the captain of the Syrian army and even though he didn't know God, God still used him to bring a great deliverance unto the people of Syria. We need to understand that the angels of the Lord only encamp around those who fear God. However, because God knows that appointed day and time when we are going to accept Jesus Christ as Our Lord and Saviour, God assigns grace and mercy to follow us. So, even though Naaman did not know the Lord, God still used him for God's purposes. The same way we were used when we were in the world; when we accept Jesus Christ as Our Lord and Saviour, God will use those things for His Kingdom. Deuteronomy 1:30, "The Lord your God which goeth before you, he shall fight for you, according to all that he did for you in Egypt before your eyes." Naaman had great favor with the King of Syria, he was known to be a mighty man of valour and he also was very wealthy but notice that the Word of God says he was a leper. Now leprosy represents the sin in our lives such as bitterness, unforgiveness, anger, pornography, or anything that goes against Our Holy God. Meanwhile, a little Jewish girl that had been taken away captive was a maid for Naaman's wife. This little girl didn't look at her situation, it didn't matter to her that she was in captivity. Her only concern was that people would hear the Gospel. For the Gospel is simple. She told her mistress, "Haven't you heard that there is a Prophet in Samaria (A Prophet in Florida or _____ from your city) that moves in the Power of God and I know that if Naaman would go to him God would heal him." Now look at the simplicity of the Gospel. God used this little girl to Preach the Good News. So, Naaman understanding the protocols, the governments and the order of things, understood that he needed to go to the King of Syria to get permission to be sent out. This is the same for us in a five fold ministry. We need to understand and follow the ways and order of Our God. See, God the Father sent His Son; Jesus sent the Holy Spirit; the Holy Spirit sent the Apostles; and the Apostles send out the Prophets, Evangelist, Pastors, and Teachers. Let's read II Kings 5-7, "And the king of Syria said, Go to, go, and I will send a letter unto the king of Israel. And he departed, and took with him ten talents of silver, and six thousand pieces of gold, and ten changes of raiment. And he brought the letter to the king of Israel, saying, now when this letter is come unto thee behold, I have therewith sent Naaman my servant to thee, that thou mayest recover him of his leprosy. And it came to pass, when the king of Israel had read the letter, that he rent his clothes, and said, "Am I God, to kill and to make alive, that this man doth send unto me to recover a man of his leprosy? Wherefore consider, I pray you, and see how he seeketh a quarrel against me." So Naaman was sent out by the King of Syria and notice he took with him gifts. See Naaman understood the principles of God that when you come to see a man or woman of God you come bringing a gift. But look what happens when Naaman presents the letter to the King of Israel. The King of Israel said, 'Am I God that I can heal someone?" Notice this people of God, The King of Israel was suppose to be the leader of God's people but because he didn't know his God, because he wasn't spending time in the Word of God, neither did he know the Power of his God, so he rent his clothes and said "Am I God?" Are we spending that time with Our God? Prophet Elisha was an awesome, powerful Prophet of God and he moved in such an awesome dimension of the spirit that he heard and knew what the King of Israel had said and done. Prophet Elisha didn't need the newspaper or even to watch the evening news; he was a Prophet separated for God moving in the realm of the spirit that God revealed all things to him. So, he said don't they know there is a Prophet among them that knows who his God is and knew his God is the Healer. II Kings 5:8-10, "And it was so, when Elisha the man of God had heard that the king of Israel had rent his clothes that he sent to the kings, saying, Wherefore hast thou rent thy clothes: let him come now to me, and he shall know that there is a prophet in Israel. So Naaman came with his horses and with his chariot, and stood at the door of the house of Elisha. And Elisha sent a messenger unto him, saying, Go and wash in Jordan seven times, and thy flesh shall come again to thee, and thou shalt be clean." So, he sent word to Naaman. This is how we have to be for our God, READY and knowing who Our God is so that people that need deliverance or healing can receive it from the Spirit of the Living God. Naaman went to see Prophet Elisha and when he got there the Prophet sent his servant out to give the Word because the Prophet was in the presence of the Lord. Naaman, being a man of authority, got offended and I believe he was thinking to himself, "Doesn't this guy know who I am, at least he could have come out himself to see me; and then he tells me to go take a bath." We need to remember the Gospel is simple and we all can preach it. Prophet Elisha knew the

Word of God; he knew that all he had to do was send forth God's Word. Psalm 107:20, "He sent his word, and healed them, and delivered them from their destruction." II Kings 5:11-14, But Naaman was wroth and went away, and said, Behold I thought, He will surely come out to me, and stand, and call on the name of the Lord his God, and strike his hand over the place and recover the leper. Are not Abana and Pharpar, rivers of Damascus, better than all the waters of Israel? May I not wash in them, and be clean? So he turned and went away in rage. And his servants came near, and spake unto him, and said, My father, if the prophet had bid thee do some great thing, wouldest thou not have done it? How much rather then, when he saith to thee Wash, and be clean? Naaman began reasoning; aren't the rivers in Damascus cleaner than the Jordan and he wants me to take a bath in the Jordan River. When we start putting our thoughts into what God says it doesn't work. Like the Word of God says in Zechariah 4:6, "....Not by might, nor by power, but by my spirit, saith the Lord of hosts." In frustration Naaman began to leave. However, again the Lord shows how simple the Gospel is and Naaman's servant began speaking to him. His servant told him if he had told you to do some hard thing wouldn't you have done it; instead he told you to do something so easy. Remember the Word says in II Chronicles 20:20; "....Believe in the Lord your God, so shall ye be established; believe his prophets, so shall ye prosper." So, Naaman went to the Jordan River and dipped himself seven times. The Word shows us this for a reason; the first time Naaman dipped he got rid of offence, the second pride, the third bitterness, the fourth unforgiveness, etc. Then after the seventh time; the number seven represents completion; Naaman came up Healed and Delivered with his skin like a newborn baby. John 3:3 says, "...Verily, verily, I say unto thee, Except a man be born again, he cannot see the kingdom of God." Then Naaman returned to Prophet Elisha to give him the gifts he had brought with him. However, the Prophet would not accept them because Naaman had waited to give the gift. In other words, instead of giving a gift of faith he was rewarding the Prophet. God can't be bought and we can never pay Our God for all He has done for us. II Kings 5:15-18, "And he returned to the man of God, he and all his company, and came, and stood before him: and said, Behold, now I know that there is no God in all the earth, but in Israel: now therefore, I pray thee, take a blessing of thy servant. But he said, As the Lord liveth, befoe whom I stand, I will receive none. And he urged him to take it, but he refuse. And Naaman said, Shall there not then, I pray thee, be given to thy servant two mules' burden of the earth? For thy servant will henceforth offer neither burnt offering nor sacrifice unto other gods, but unto the Lord. In this thing the Lord pardon thy servant, that when my master goeth into the house of Rimmon to worship there, and he leaneth on my hand, and I bow myself in the house of Rimmon: when I bow down myself in the house of Rimmon, the Lord pardon thy servant in this thing." I believe when Naaman was being washed by the Water he must have left a hand or his tongue out, because he was excusing himself when he began saying when he goes back to his king in Syria and goes into the house of Rimmon where his king worshipped to forgive him for bowing down to another god. We need to make sure everything gets dunked so we can become new; Born Again. We need to get rid of the people pleasing spirit and do what God has called us to do, PREACH THE GOSPEL OF JESUS CHRIST for it is the Power unto Salvation. The Gospel is Simple, Glory to God Forever!!

CONCLUSION

As I was waking up one morning, the Lord gave me the understanding that many people think they have waited so long for their petitions they have before the Lord. I realized that Our Lord has been waiting for over 2000 years for His Bride. As I was thinking on this, I had a vision, like a trance, of the rapture; I could see very tall mountains in the background. It looked like an orange-lit sky. Then I saw a lot of spirits rising up into the heavens. In seeing this I felt the Lord was showing me that the time was drawing near for the Bride to be taken up. The Word of God says, "For wheresoever the carcass is, there will the eagles be gathered together." (Matthew 24:28) I believe this means that the Prophets are coming to declare the Word of the Lord to bring life back to the Body of Christ. Ask yourself, do you want to be used by Our God. When it comes to spiritual things of God; how quick, how fast, and how bad we want them is all up to us. Are we willing to pay the price, to lay down our lives for Him and fulfill the call of God in our lives? Get what the Lord Jesus has for your life by being separated unto Him, seeking His Face and loving on Him.

As a Prophet of God, I speak the Blessings of the Lord Jesus Christ over your life. "The Lord bless thee, and keep thee: the Lord make his face shine upon thee, and be gracious unto thee: the Lord lift up his countenance upon thee, and give thee peace." Numbers 6:24-26.

Contact Information:
www. EnFuegoforJesus.com
EnFuegoforJesus Ministry
P.O. Box 730777
Ormond Beach, FL 32173-0777

CPSIA information can be obtained
at www.ICGtesting.com
Printed in the USA
LVHW091253220219
608459LV00001B/41/P